McCORMICK
Mystery of Lord Kit…

So that your telephone call is charged at local rate,
please call the numbers as set out below:

	From Area codes 01923 or 0208:	From the rest of Herts:
Renewals:	01923 471373	01438 737373
Enquiries:	01923 471333	01438 737333
Minicom:	01923 471599	01438 737599

L32b

THE MYSTERY OF
LORD KITCHENER'S DEATH

The Mystery of
LORD KITCHENER'S
DEATH

By

DONALD McCORMICK

PUTNAM
42 GREAT RUSSELL STREET
LONDON

B09 06038

Made and printed in Great Britain by
W. & J. Mackay & Co Ltd, Chatham
for the publishers, Putnam & Co Ltd.

Contents

Illustrations

1

A Day When Nothing Went Right

A GAUNT, commanding figure paced up and down the platform of King's Cross Station in London on the evening of Sunday, 4 June, 1916.

Few people were about and none seemed to be paying the slightest attention to him. He might well have been any senior officer waiting to catch a train. Yet a quick glance at the face above the red tabs, with its unmistakable moustache rampant, would have revealed that this was Field-Marshal Earl Kitchener of Khartoum, Secretary of State for War in His Majesty's Government, perhaps, by reason of the celebrated recruiting poster, the most easily recognised man in all Britain.

No special precautions seemed to have been taken to keep his movements secret. Private Dunckley, of the Royal West Kent Regiment, had wandered on to the platform in error: he had mistaken King's Cross Station for nearby St. Pancras and no one had stopped him.

'Got the shock of my life when I saw Lord Kitchener plumb in front of me. Nearly forgot to salute. But I cut him off one at the last moment. And he returned it. He looked absent-minded and tired. There's a sick man, I said to myself.'

Others noticed Kitchener, too. There was Alfred Burnden, a porter, who 'thought it odd that nobody was bothering about his lordship. I nearly asked him if I could be of any help, but somehow he looked a little too forbidding for me to do that.'

Nevertheless porter Burnden stopped to ask a station official whether he knew who the officer was. And was promptly rebuffed.

'It was none of my business, I was told,' said Burnden ruefully. 'They didn't even provide a private waiting-room for him, which was something they always did for the politicians when they went by train anywhere. Cor blimey, you would think they wanted to advertise he was making a trip!'

For porter Burnden it was a day when nothing went right. For two hours he didn't pick up a single tip.

For many others, too, it was a day of misadventure. While Kitchener was left to pace the platform alone, members of his entourage and station officials were frantically telephoning for information on a Very Important Personage indeed. Not a general, or a politician, but a mere servant. For while the party could have set off without the servant, it could not have fulfilled its mission without the cipher which he was carrying.

Mr. H. J. O'Beirne, of the Foreign Office, was to accompany the War Minister to Scotland. But, to his consternation, he learned on arriving at King's Cross that his servant had failed to join him. According to Sir George Arthur, Lord Kitchener's biographer, this man had been misdirected to another station and his failure to appear had 'left his master cipherless'. It is surprising that a Foreign Office man should have entrusted his cipher to anyone on the eve of so important a mission, let alone to such an inefficient person as this servant.

Eventually, a few minutes before the train was due to leave, the man was located and it was arranged that he and Mr. O'Beirne should follow on by a special train. The servant's excuse was that just before he set off for King's Cross he had received a telephone message from an unknown person asking him to go to Marylebone Station where he would be met by a 'Colonel Datchett'. No one had heard of Colonel Datchett and his identity remains a mystery to this day.

Meanwhile at King's Cross Station the party assembled alongside the train. Besides Lord Kitchener there were Brigadier-

General W. Ellershaw, Lieutenant-Colonel O. A. Fitzgerald (the War Minister's Military Secretary), 2nd Lieutenant R. D. Macpherson (a young officer acting as interpreter for the party), Sir H. F. Donaldson and Mr. L. S. Robertson, of the Ministry of Munitions, Detective Inspector MacLaughlin, of Scotland Yard, two servants, Mr. Henry Surguy-Shields and Mr. Walter Gurney, and Driver D. C. Brown, of the Royal Horse Artillery. They were about to embark on the first stage of a mission to Petrograd at the invitation of Czar Nicholas of Russia, who, seriously perturbed at the way the war was going on the eastern front, urgently wanted talks with the British War Minister.

In the last moments before departure Kitchener appeared to some to be silent and saturnine. Possibly he was annoyed at the blunder of Mr. O'Beirne's servant and puzzled about the mysterious 'Colonel Datchett'. But onlookers thought they detected an unusual tenseness and a nervousness which as a rule this very tough soldier never showed. He was 'abnormally agitated and anxious'* as he strode impatiently backwards and forwards on the platform. Every few seconds he 'peered over his shoulder as though he was looking for somebody,' testified porter Burnden. Even his farewells were more solemn than usual: they had about them an air of finality.

On the other hand Colonel Sir Henry Creedy, of the War Office, who with Sir George Arthur and others was there to see him off, did not notice anything unusual about the War Minister. 'He may have felt that this mission was one way of getting him away from the War Office for a period, and certainly he did not wish to be away for long. But he was quite calm and businesslike,' said Sir Henry.

Yet he seemed reluctant to enter his compartment. He gave a final glance down the platform and when one of the party asked whether he wanted anything, replied brusquely: 'I was expecting someone. He has failed to turn up.' Then he shrugged his shoulders and stepped aboard the train. Immediately he

*Sir George Arthur.

opened his dispatch case and immersed himself in his papers. He did not trouble to look up again even when the train steamed out of the station on its 700 miles journey to Thurso.

As soon as the train left King's Cross a telegram was sent in cipher to the Commander-in-Chief at Scapa Flow, informing him that the party had left and would arrive at Thurso on the forenoon of the following day.

Of more interest is the dispatch which that very evening Walter Page, the United States Ambassador in London, was writing to Washington, making this observation:

'There is (in England) a hope and feeling that he (Kitchener) may not come back from Russia.'*

From so well informed, astute and accurate an observer as Page, this was indeed a remarkable comment. What is, however, even more remarkable is that Page, the Ambassador of a then neutral nation, should know all about this supposedly top-secret mission.

*   *   *   *   *

The weather deteriorated as the train headed north. Gusts of wind beat incessantly against the windows and the wind rose ominously. By early morning on June 5, on its arrival at Thurso, the barometer was falling rapidly and a big sea was running.

In his headquarters aboard the flagship *Iron Duke*, Admiral Sir John Jellicoe, the Commander-in-Chief, was beset with many problems. First he had to assess the full implications of the Battle of Jutland, which had just been fought. This meant weighing heavy British naval losses against the unknown state of the German Grand Fleet. Had their ships been mauled so badly that, as a fighting unit, they would never venture forth *en masse* again? Secondly, he had to report to the Admiralty on his considerable losses in men and ships. Thirdly, he was confronted with the task of re-organising the battle cruiser and cruiser squadrons. Finally, there were the arrangements for Lord Kitchener's mission to Russia. It is not surprising that he

*Correspondence of Walter Page.

was a harassed man. For him, too, nothing had gone right in the past twenty-four hours and now he had bad weather as well to contend with.

Originally, Admiral Sir Henry Oliver, then Chief of Staff, had arranged for Kitchener to embark in the cruiser *Hampshire* on the Clyde. But the War Minister had expressed a wish to visit the Grand Fleet at Scapa Flow on his way to Russia. So Oliver ordered the *Hampshire* to Scapa Flow and went over to the War Office to tell the Minister personally the time of the special train to Thurso and the revised travelling arrangements.*

For some reason Kitchener still demurred at the proposals. He wanted to go on board the *Hampshire* at Thurso and sail in her to Scapa Flow. But the Commander-in-Chief, on being consulted, did not consider this desirable, owing to the risk of submarine attack, and telegraphed on June 4 that it would be safer for the crossing to be made in a destroyer.

On the morning of June 5 Kitchener and his party crossed from Thurso in H.M.S. *Oak*, the servants and luggage being accommodated in the Fleet messenger *Alouette*. Mr. O'Beirne and his servant, Mr. C. L. Rix, rejoined the mission at Scapa Flow. The War Minister lunched aboard the *Iron Duke* with Jellicoe and other Flag Officers present. 'During lunch he discussed with me his forthcoming trip,' wrote Jellicoe, 'and said once or twice that he was looking forward to it as a real holiday. The strain of the last two years, he confessed, had been very great, and he had felt that he could not have gone on without this break, which he heartily welcomed.

'Lord Kitchener impressed me strongly with the idea that he was working to a timetable, and that he felt he had not a day to lose. He mentioned three weeks as the limit of his absence, and I expressed astonishment at the programme which he had planned to carry out in the restricted period.

'He was most anxious not to lose a moment of the sea trip

*Extracts from the diary of Admiral of the Fleet Sir Henry Oliver (see Admiral James's biography).

and asked me more than once what I thought was the shortest time in which the passage could be made.'*

Doubtless, as the weather worsened, Jellicoe's instinct must have been to persuade Kitchener to agree to postponing sailing. But the War Minister would brook no delay. The gale was blowing from the north-east and the route which had been planned for the *Hampshire* was that which passed up the eastern side of Orkney, following the channel which was normally searched by mine-sweeping vessels as a routine measure. But, as the sea was heaviest on the eastern side, not only was mine-sweeping out of the question, but it was obvious that escorting destroyers could not possibly keep up with the high speed of the cruiser in such a swell.

So, at the last moment, Jellicoe decided to scrap this plan, and to discuss with his staff which route on the western and lee side of the islands would be safest. As a result of these discussions it was agreed that the *Hampshire* should pass close inshore and not take the alternative route farther to the west, near Sule Skerry Lighthouse.

The arguments in favour of this course were that the sea would not be so heavy on this route and that there would be more chance of the escort keeping up with the *Hampshire*. Also, as the route was one used by Fleet auxiliaries, it was under close observation.

Error, ill luck and bad judgement, however, continued to provide a catalogue of misadventures in the twenty-four hours between the commencement of the mission's journey from London and the issuing of sailing orders to the *Hampshire*'s captain.

'Those who made the weather forecast aboard the *Iron Duke*, on which the decision to sail was based, didn't understand what type of "storm structure" prevailed at the time,' declared Mr. A. G. McAdie, professor of meteorology at Harvard University.†

The Grand Fleet: 1914–16 by Admiral of the Fleet Viscount Jellicoe of Scapa.

† *War Weather Vignettes*, by A. G. McAdie.

Yet the indications were all there. A clearly defined and well-known type of cyclone was passing from the Atlantic to the North Sea and about to recurve before heading north-west into the Arctic regions. 'The counsel of the weather-wise,' added McAdie, 'would have been to wait and follow the depression rather than to try to precede it. It was not a scientific forecast.'

Naval meteorological forecasts have been inaccurate on many critical occasions. One suspects that far too often junior officers undertaking such work have tended to say 'Yes' rather than 'No' to impatient flag officers anxious to send ships to sea.

Summing up the problem of deciding the *Hampshire*'s route, Admiral Jellicoe wrote afterwards: 'It was practically impossible that this route could have been mined owing to the dark period in northern latitudes being confined to a couple of hours, during which no ship could expect to approach the shore and complete her mine-laying without being sighted. . . . Mine-laying by enemy submarines had been confined to waters well to the southward of the Firth of Forth, presumably because of their small radius of action.'

This statement shows a certain complacency on the part of Jellicoe. As was later admitted by the Admiralty: 'The waters in the vicinity of the ordinary eastern exit used by the Fleet were frequently visited by enemy submarines. One had appeared there less than a week before (i.e. before June 5) and had fired a torpedo at one of the Fleet minesweeping vessels and been hunted without success by destroyers. Another had been reported just west of Pentland Skerries, i.e. in the eastern entrance, on the morning of June 3. At the time . . . there was good reason for considering both the eastern and western channels as under suspicion.'

Did Jellicoe know of all this, and yet not realise the extent of the risk? As the gale had hindered mine-sweeping operations at a time when German mine-laying was constantly being carried out in these waters, it would have seemed advisable to delay the sailing of the *Hampshire* for at least forty-eight hours.

Admiral Sir Lionel Preston, who was at that time in command of Fleet minesweepers, makes this comment: 'I was in daily touch with the Chief of Staff, Admiral Madden, and on every occasion (other than the case of the unfortunate *Hampshire*) I conferred as to swept channels. On this occasion I knew nothing of the arrival of Kitchener and the decision to use the actual channel was made in the flagship.

'There were three swept entrances to Scapa Flow: the East Channel, the West Channel and what was termed the North-West Triangle.

'On that morning I was ordered to sweep the West Channel. It was blowing half a gale and the sweep was difficult. I reported that the sweep was unsatisfactory. As we slipped one sweep a submarine was sighted and duly reported.

'On the strength of my report Admiral Jellicoe evidently decided to use the North-West Triangle. This channel was seldom swept, but it was throughout used as the entrance channel for merchant ships and a constant flow of traffic went through it unharmed.'

*   *   *   *   *

A cruiser of the County, or Devonshire class of 10,850 tons displacement, H.M.S. *Hampshire* was laid down in September, 1902, and first commissioned in August, 1905. Thus, at the time of this story, she was eleven years old. She may not have measured up completely in war-worthiness to those cruisers completed in the boom building years immediately prior to the war, but the allegation that she would have been scrapped before 1916, but for the war, is unfounded.

The German General Wetzell is reported to have asked Lloyd George during the latter's visit to Germany in the nineteen-thirties: 'I have always wondered why the British Government sent Kitchener to sea in such an out-dated cruiser as the *Hampshire*. Can you tell me the reason why?'

But the *Hampshire* was not all that outdated. For a warship she was young—a mere babe compared to such effective veterans as *Warspite*, *Renown* and *Royal Sovereign* were in World War II. Such immense strides were made in ship-building techniques between 1902 and 1914 that, it must be admitted, in some respects she was lacking essential safeguards for fighting a modern war. The advent of the mine, the accurate gun-power of German warships meant that armour-plating which was adequate in 1905 was insufficient in 1916. There was a 6-inch belt of armour amidships, 10½ feet wide and 325 feet long. The belt for'ard was 2 inch, as also was the reinforcing belt on deck, while the most vital parts of the ship were protected by a 6-inch belt. The total weight of armour was 6,665 tons.

Whereas the Germans had tended to sacrifice speed for greater armour protection, doubtless a tribute to the efficiency of British naval gunnery, the British had insisted that 'speed is armour'. This policy certainly gave British cruisers greater mobility and to some extent greater hitting power, but there were grave disadvantages in the thinness of armour.

The cruiser's armament comprised four 7.5-inch guns, six 6-inch Mark VII, two 12-pounders, twenty 3-pounders, and two submerged torpedo tubes. She carried a complement of 665.

Just before the war the *Hampshire* had completed a commission on the China Station, visiting Hong Kong, Vladivostok and the Japanese ports. She was at Wei-Hai-Wei, exercising with the rest of the China Fleet, when war broke out. Within a few weeks she was joining in the hunt for the German raider *Emden* in eastern waters, varying the routine of a ship on active service with occasional visits to islands of the Indian Ocean, where she took aboard cargoes of fruit and coconuts, and, on one occasion, four goats which became ship's mascots. These succumbed to the cold when the *Hampshire* sailed for more northerly waters, but became a legend which the ship's company were never allowed to live down; the arrival of the ship in any home port was greeted with ribald 'baas' from sailors in other ships, interlarded with Rabelaisian allegations about the reason for the unusual cargo.

L.K.D.—B

Prisoners and survivors from the *Emden* were brought by the cruiser from the Far East to Malta. Then, after a Christmas spent in Gibraltar, the ship commissioned with a Portsmouth crew and was ordered to Devonport.

This did not meet with the approval of the Portsmouth-based ship's company. In those days not only was there intense rivalry between the major naval bases of Chatham, Devonport and Portsmouth, but there was a marked dislike among lower deck men from Chatham and Portsmouth for their opposite numbers at Devonport. The latter included a large percentage of Cornishmen, who were regarded as hostile 'foreigners' and the Devonport petty officers had a reputation for being harsh taskmasters.

This incident, small in itself, helped, as far as one can gather at a distance of more than forty years, to give the *Hampshire* the undeserved nickname of a 'jinx ship'. Sailors are often superstitious, and the orders detaching the cruiser to Devonport were looked upon, stupidly perhaps, as an ill omen.

In the early days of the war the *Hampshire* was one of the fastest ships in the Royal Navy, capable of 23 knots. After leaving Devonport she sailed for Scapa Flow and joined the Grand Fleet in 1915, dividing her time between the main base and Invergordon. She was constantly in action, first with the Sixth Cruiser Squadron, later off Moray Firth, where she was nearly torpedoed.

A story gained credence in the twenties that the *Hampshire* with Lord Kitchener aboard had been attacked by a submarine in the Mediterranean earlier in the war, and that a spy was shot for signalling to the submarine. This was quite untrue. The cruiser had not been on the Mediterranean Station during the war, except on passage from the Far East, and Lord Kitchener had not embarked in her since 1912, when he sailed in the ship from Egypt to Malta and back.

The ship in which he embarked in the Mediterranean during the war was H.M.S. *Dartmouth*, and the only recorded attack on the *Hampshire* by a submarine was that in the Moray Firth already mentioned. That was on July 1, 1915, when U25 unsuccessfully fired a torpedo at her.

Later the cruiser helped to protect the White Sea trade route, coaling at Alexandrovsk. She had, it was true, her share of bad luck. When in quest of the *Emden*, whom her ship's company had sworn that they alone would capture, she ran out of fuel. Her normal coaling capacity was 800 tons, with a maximum of 1,800. She also had frequent mechanical trouble, and changing conditions of warfare had enforced refits. She had to be overhauled at Birkenhead, and later, on Admiralty instructions, was ordered to Belfast so that her main deck guns could be mounted on the upper deck. During World War I there was a prolonged controversy over the positioning of guns, with the gunnery experts demanding that they should be placed as high as possible above the water line, while designers insisted that this made for top heaviness and reduced speed. During this refit it was rumoured that spies had been found aboard the cruiser, an allegation which will be examined in detail in another chapter. There had also been frequent changes of personnel, and factors such as these, coupled with the Devonport incident, quite unjustifiably, gave the cruiser the legend of being 'a bit of a hoodoo'.

Then in May 1916, came the *Hampshire*'s greatest hour. Morale was high as she sailed with the rest of the Grand Fleet to take part in the Battle of Jutland, the last of the great sea battles of this century, with Captain Herbert J. Savill in command. She acted as linking ship between the cruiser squadrons and the Battle Fleet before the action, and during this period reached a speed of 21 knots. On May 30 she sighted an enemy submarine, which she rammed and sank.

Captain Savill had had a distinguished career in the Navy, having been a lieutenant in the Naval Brigade during the Boer War, and at one time Commander of the Royal Naval College at Greenwich.

On the ship's return to Scapa Flow after Jutland, orders were received to 'provision ship' immediately; the following day,

June 4, a signal from the Commander-in-Chief instructed Captain Savill to anchor in a position close to the *Iron Duke*. This order caused a flutter of excitement among the crew. A mess deck buzz circulated the news that there was 'a very special job' to be undertaken.

As the cruiser took up her new anchorage the weather worsened. While the cable was being connected to the buoy, the ship's blacksmith lost his foothold in the gale-force wind and his leg was jammed by the ring of the cable. When the injured man was at last freed from his predicament, he was found to be so seriously hurt that his leg had to be amputated. So he was rushed over to the hospital ship *Soudan*, where an operation was performed.

This was the only mishap in this chapter of accidents which, in the final reckoning, proved a blessing for somebody—in this case the blacksmith himself.

On that forenoon of June 5 there was more excitement than grumbling on the part of the men as they set about cleaning ship. They turned to readily enough and supplied that extra touch of spit and polish which the First Lieutenant had indicated was highly desirable. As they swabbed the decks, the seamen exchanged gossip about the hints of a 'hush-hush mission'.

'With the exception of the captain, we aboard the *Hampshire* had no knowledge of the nature of the special mission that Admiralty orders of the previous evening had informed us the ship was to undertake,' said Stoker Walter Farnden. 'Neither the officers nor the men had any idea of the identity of the "distinguished person" who, it was rumoured, was to be a passenger.'

The lower deck's bush telegraph system, whether by intuition or by deduction, is usually up-to-date with its news. 'At 3 p.m. on June 5,' stated Chief Shipwright William Charles Phillips, 'we heard that Lord Kitchener was coming with us.'

He did not disclose how he heard. Few others could have known, and it was with considerable curiosity that the crew awaited the arrival of the pinnace from the *Iron Duke* that afternoon.

'It's a big nob all right,' whispered a seaman as, shortly after four o'clock, the Commander-in-Chief's pinnace was seen bustling across the Flow towards the cruiser.

As the craft came nearer it was possible by telescope to distinguish a number of khaki-clad figures in the boat.

'God help us all!' muttered a leading signalman, putting down his binoculars. 'A shower of perishin' brasshats. If that doesn't mean trouble, I'll shave off.'

'Rubbish,' commented Leading Seaman Rogerson. 'We're as lucky as any ship afloat. So far we've dodged every torpedo fired at us, and we didn't have a single casualty at Jutland.'

It was true. During the Battle of Jutland the *Hampshire* was one of the luckiest ships in action. She sank at least one submarine—some said two—but, though shells were rained all round her, she was not hit once.

'Stop dripping,* killick,' muttered another signalman. 'Can't you see who it is coming aboard? It's the bloody old Chief Recruitin' Officer 'isself. Just the spit image of 'is bleedin' poster!'

'Well, if it's K. himself, we're as safe as if we were in barracks,' added another.

But now the pinnace was alongside, rising and falling like a cork in the heavy swell. Seamen in sou-westers and oilskins grappled with hawsers in the blinding rain and roaring wind as Captain Savill stood at the top of the gangway to greet Lord Kitchener and his party.

There was one last mishap that afternoon before they sailed. A seaman, who had been examining an engagement ring he had bought for his fiancée, dropped it over the ship's side in his excitement at the War Minister's arrival. He had had that ring in his possession for eighteen months, but had never had a chance of giving it to his betrothed.

*'Dripping' is navalese for 'moaning'. 'Killick' is slang for a leading rating.

2

'Make Way for Lord Kitchener'

AT the very last moment before Kitchener left the *Iron Duke*, Admiral Jellicoe, who was having increasing doubts about the risks involved, once again tried to persuade the Field-Marshal to wait twenty-four hours. But Kitchener was adamant. He had no time to lose. There was urgent business to be discussed in Russia and a delay of even a day might ruin his chances of success.

'But, sir, if you will only give us time to make a satisfactory sweep of the channel,' pleaded the Commander-in-Chief.

Kitchener, however, pointed out, quite rightly, that there were no signs of the storm abating, that, if anything, it was getting worse. And, he added, the sweepers probably would not be able to start operations for another twenty-four hours. In this case a postponement of sailing might mean a delay of two days.

Should Jellicoe have sent a message to the Admiralty indicating his doubts? With so much at stake and with the knowledge of unswept seas ahead, perhaps he should have done so. How their lordships in Whitehall would have received the message is another question. The Commander-in-Chief must have known that they were far too occupied with reports on Jutland to wish to be bothered with a query about sailing orders.

Once Kitchener and his party were aboard no time was lost. Within half an hour the *Hampshire* slipped her buoy and at

4.45 p.m. was under way. At 5.30 p.m. she steamed towards Hoy through the western exit from Scapa Flow.

Meanwhile two destroyers, *Unity* and *Victor*, had left an hour and a half earlier to search the waters off Hoy on the route which the *Hampshire* was to follow. At 5.45 p.m. they picked up the cruiser off Tor Ness and, acting under orders, escorted her along the western coast of Orkney.

Kitchener retired to the Captain's cabin, accompanied by Lieutenant-Colonel Fitzgerald and 2nd Lieutenant Macpherson, of the Cameronians. During the Jutland action the cabin had been transformed into a War Station Room, and its tables covered with charts and movement plots of the Grand Fleet. Only the previous day had all this been cleared away and the cabin made ready for its new occupant.

Above decks everything possible had been battened down; hatches and scuttles were fastened, all loose gear and tackle secured and lashed to the decks. As the cruiser rounded Stromness she faced the full force of the gale. Wind and rain cut the faces of those above decks, and the hands on the fo'c'sle were drenched to the skin as wave upon wave crashed over the bows.

'It was,' said Petty Officer Wilfred Wesson, 'the most terrific gale in my experience. The wind had suddenly veered round to north-west. It whipped the sea to a fury.'

The change in the wind was unexpected and it upset the calculations of those who had expected an easier passage along the western side of Orkney.

'We hung on like grim death to prevent ourselves being thrown off,' said Chief Shipwright Phillips.

Unity and *Victor* laboured gallantly but ineffectually in the wake of the fast moving cruiser. She was, despite the weather, pounding through the heavy seas at 18 knots. The signal logs of the destroyers afterwards showed that, on picking them up, the *Hampshire* ordered a speed of 18 knots to be maintained. At times both destroyers seemed to disappear beneath the waves; once *Victor* swung violently off course as she was almost pooped.

As the wind moaned like a banshee and shook the rigging as if it would tear it to shreds, cascades of foaming, green seas poured over the decks of the *Hampshire*. Captain Savill twisted on his stool and looked astern at the plight of the two destroyers, pitching and tossing as they gallantly strove to hold their course. It did not take long for him to decide that it was practically impossible for them to keep up with the cruiser in a storm such as this. Either he must order *Hampshire* to reduce speed, which would make her an easier target for submarines, or she must push on without an escort.

Soon after 6 p.m. the Yeoman of Signals crossed the bridge, saluted smartly and reported: 'Signal from *Unity*, sir. Repeated from *Victor*. "*Victor to Unity: can only make speed of fifteen knots*", sir.'

'Acknowledge,' said the captain. Then, turning to the navigation officer: 'Starboard five. Revolutions for sixteen knots.'

Bending down so that his mouth was close up against the voice-pipe, thus ensuring that his words would carry despite the noise of the gale, the navigating officer repeated the captain's orders.

Deep down below, where there was little chance of an enemy shell hitting him, the quarter-master stood, legs well apart, hands on the wheel, his ears straining for the next order. He had only just come on duty for the second dog watch and had barely had time to accustom himself to the struggle of holding the huge ship on an even course in the face of the violent head wind. It was almost a relief to take his eye off the compass for a moment as he replied 'Starboard five, sir,' before spinning the wheel to his right. Then, as the indicator swung over, he added: 'Five of starboard wheel on, sir.'

We must be going closer into land, thought the quarter-master, as the navigating officer called 'Midships' and he steadied up on a new course. And he grinned as he wondered how the Secretary of State for War was feeling in this weather.

Captain Savill's first impulse was to reduce speed to sixteen knots and to carry on with *Unity* alone, ordering *Victor* to return to base. But even while this message was being passed, *Unity*, too, had found herself in difficulties and signalled her inability to maintain a speed of more than twelve knots.

The telegraphman had rung down for the reduction of speed in the engine room as the quartermaster repeated the change in revolutions. They guessed that the destroyers were having difficulty in keeping up with the cruiser, for they knew from the uneven roll of the ship that, as the quartermaster remarked, 'above decks it must be a proper bastard tonight.'

In a big ship the men below decks are as isolated from what is happening outside as the prisoner in his cell is cut off from the world beyond the walls. Neither the quartermaster nor the telegraphman could know that *Unity* and *Victor* were dropping farther and farther astern. Each was more concerned with the chance of a smoother passage as the cruiser edged closer to the shore. The quartermaster hoped he might eat his supper in relative comfort.

Only the orders which filtered through to them down the voice-pipe gave any indication of the way things were going in the world above. And within a few minutes another order came down: 'Reduce to fifteen knots.'

At the same time Captain Savill cancelled his previous signal to *Victor*, then sent this message to *Unity*: 'I am only going fifteen knots. Can you keep up?'

But *Victor* was by this time only making ten knots in the face of the rapidly increasing gale, and was forced to reply in the negative.

Captain Savill left his stool and crossed the bridge. Once more he focused his binoculars on the two destroyers, forlornly like fragments of matchwood in the maelstrom which the sea had become. They were now so far astern of the cruiser that they were barely discernible specks on the raging seas; more often than not they were lost to sight in a trough of waves.

'Better signal them now before we lose visual contact,' decided the captain. 'They will be quite useless in these conditions. It is senseless for them to carry on.'

There was no other decision at which he could reasonably have arrived. He dared not risk reducing speed again. Accordingly at 6.20 p.m. *Hampshire* signalled to *Unity* 'Destroyers return to base', repeating the order to *Victor* at 6.30 p.m. These signals were duly recorded in the signal logs of the destroyers. Faint, blinking lights indicated that the message had been 'received and understood'. Flashing a final 'Good luck' message, the destroyers turned back to Scapa.

Now the cruiser was going it alone against the elements, relying on her speed, her armament and the fact that this was not a warship route to carry her through safely. But weather conditions made it impossible for her to make full use of her speed. And Captain Savill, with that chivalry which seasoned sailors so often and so tolerantly show towards the mere land-lubber, was concerned about Lord Kitchener's comfort. He had been shocked to see how ill and tired the War Minister was looking when he arrived aboard the cruiser, and he worried more because he had been carefully briefed about Kitchener's proneness to seasickness and the agonies he suffered from it.

Anxious to do anything he could to alleviate such suffering, Captain Savill decided that, to allow his distinguished passenger to eat his dinner in at least a slightly less disagreeable state of discomfort, he would leave the charted channel and go closer to the land. By hugging the coast of Orkney, he hoped to get some semblance of a lee.

So the ship veered off towards the grim, bleak towers of black rock that rose sheerly against the sky line. Barely two miles to starboard was the death-dealing coastline of Orkney, a vast expanse of unbroken cliff, pin-pointed at intervals by razor-edged rocks jutting out to sea and forming a natural barrier against any attempt to land on this desolate, melancholy territory. The *Hampshire* kept as close in to this forbidding coast as was navigationally safe.

Between 7.30 and 7.40 p.m. the cruiser was in a position about one and a half miles from the shore between the Brough of Birsay and Marwick Head, shaping a course N. 30° E.

Though so close inshore, there was a depth of more than 30 fathoms here. The ship's speed was between 13 and 15 knots. Nevertheless, with the wind now north-west, there was very little protection from the gale. As the 'Hands to supper' bugle sounded above the shrieking of the tempest, those who had been on duty above decks were glad to seek some relative peace and warmth below.

Petty Officer Wesson went down to the mess deck.

'What about Leicester Square tonight?' asked Tom Leach, who, like Wesson, was a Londoner.

'Even Leicester Square would be empty on a night like this,' chipped in another. 'Every tart in the West End would be sunk without trace.'

Leach munched his bread and cheese with a grunt. 'Well, I'd swap this coast for it any time,' he added wistfully.

'Trust this old tub to run into trouble. That's her middle name,' said another. 'Bet the brasshats are as sick as dogs.'

Then Samuel Sweeney, another petty officer, started a conversation about the risks of submarines round this coast.

'Nonsense, we're too fast for 'em.'

'Fast we may be, but not in a sea like this. Besides in this weather you'd never see a torpedo track. We'd be hit before we knew what was coming to us.'

'And in a sea like this a submarine wouldn't stand a chance of accurate aim with the ship yawing like a fishing smack at anchor.'

'Weather's too bad for 'em. No U-boat would venture far on a night like this.'

Someone else suggested that mines were the only danger. He, too, was shouted down as an alarmist.

In the petty officers' mess Chief Shipwright Phillips and a few others were preparing to have a game of cards. They were experienced sailors and unaffected by the storm. Just as the first hand was being dealt a messenger appeared with instructions for Phillips to get the key of the storeroom to issue bedding for Lord Kitchener and his staff.

Phillips, thinking it was rather late in the day to be issuing bedding, put down his cards and hurried off. Presumably some pampered Army officer had complained of the cold and the Commander had decided extra blankets should be given out. The Army always were a crowd of frowsters, thought Phillips, as he went to the sentry in charge of the keyboard and told him what he wanted.

The Marine sentry grimaced, then turned to open the cabinet. 'At that very moment,' said Phillips, 'a terrific blast went through the ship. The keyboard smashed to pieces at our feet.'

There was a deadened explosion and a rush of hot air, as though the doors of some outsize oven had been opened. 'Then I smelt fumes . . . they were unmistakably the fumes one associates with a mine.'

Petty Officer Wesson recalled that about 8 p.m. someone had just mentioned that the channel had been swept for mines (not that any of those in the mess decks were justified in making such an assertion, for they couldn't possibly know). 'Those were the last words I heard just before it happened. The watch below were standing by their hammocks ready to turn in when the explosion occurred.

'You could hear it above the noise of the gale. The ship lurched. There was a dreadful grating sound somewhere in the bowels of the vessel, like flints flung into machinery.'

Wesson's memory was at fault. As far as can be ascertained from conflicting reports the explosion occurred between 7.40 and 7.45 p.m. The only independent evidence apart from that of survivors, came from a solitary Army look-out at Birsay, who, shortly after 8 p.m. that night, reported that a warship was in difficulties.

The blast from the explosion swept through the mess decks like a whirlwind. There was a fierce hiss of escaping steam. Accounts of the nature of the explosion varied. Some said there were two explosions simultaneously; others swore that the second followed the first at an interval of about a minute. A few argued that there were three distinct explosions. One might have been a boiler bursting.

'A rumbling explosion . . . not at all a sharp explosion There was a small one afterwards not as loud as the first,' said one man.

'It was like an electric light bulb bursting. There was very little noise,' was another's comment.

'A loud report.'

'Not a loud explosion. One heard it faintly.'

'It seemed pretty loud, like a double explosion to me.'

'Heard what sounded like a big sea hit the ship.'

'Heard one explosion.'

'The gas nearly suffocated me when I tried to get off the stoker's mess-deck.'

'An explosion similar to one or two electric light globes being broken, and later one or two explosions similar to a three-pounder gun going off. Heard two or three explosions altogether.'*

But there was no mistaking that the *Hampshire* had run into trouble and that something was seriously wrong with her. A roar of rushing water was heard aft; above decks was the thud-thud of tramping feet and the confused hubbub of shouted orders.

Many times that night the mess-deck had slanted sharply as the ship tossed and rolled, and plates and cutlery slithered off the tables. But this time there was an ominous slant that did not seem to right itself.

Then the lights flickered out, as the electric power failed. The slant of the mess-deck increased to thirty degrees and as it did so there was a hideous dragging sound aft as though everything movable was plunging wildly across the ship.

Down in the engine room men were trapped. Some of the stokers on duty on the port side were badly burned and the fumes of high explosive penetrated into the stokers' mess deck. A few struggled unavailingly to escape from the suffocating,

*Statements by survivors quoted in Admiralty White Paper.

acrid smoke, but in the darkness they had little hope of finding an exit from the charnel house which the forepart of the engine room had become.

'It was as though an express train crashed into us first one side, then the other,' said Stoker Alfred Read afterwards. 'I made sure we had been struck by a pair of mines.'

Red hot fragments of steel had been forced through a bulkhead near the engine room; men who had been alive and active a few seconds previously were no longer recognisably visible. Pulped flesh and scorched pieces of uniform were spattered on the bulkheads.

As two gunnery ratings slammed a watertight door to keep out the rushing water the screams of tormented men could be heard through a voice-pipe. Then there was silence as the water poured in and drowned those helplessly imprisoned below.

There were muttered curses as men groped and barged into one another in the pitch darkness. Men groped their way along the bulkheads trying to find a way out. Every hatch except one had been battened down. That hatch was aft; the seamen's mess deck was for'ard. The flats and compartment ways were filled with gushing water, sometimes a trickle, more often a deluge. At the companion ways there was a congested scramble to get to the upper decks.

As Petty Officer Wesson reached the half-deck someone shouted to him that the *Hampshire* had struck a mine. 'It's exploded on the port side of the foremost engine room. The boiler has burst,' called a stoker. His face was covered in blood, his uniform torn and burnt. He remembered only the flames in an alley-way and a muffled order from above to 'Flood the magazine'. He groped his way instinctively to the twin wheels which operated the inlet valves and grasped them firmly. Even as he did so he drew his hands back in pain: the wheels were scorchingly hot. Somehow he forced himself to try again and with an effort wrenched the wheels round until his hands were charred to the bone. Then, as the *Hampshire* heeled over, the valves dipped beneath the surface, providing just sufficient pressure for the sea water to well up into the magazine, thereby preventing a further disaster.

Many others reached the upper deck in a mutilated condition. A few, who had been overcome by fumes, were carried up the companion ways by their shipmates. The habit of discipline prevailed, even in the darkness.

The explosion seemed to have occurred under the forepart of the ship and probably near the keel. The signalman on the bridge said it 'tore the centre part of the ship right out of her' and that 'she started going down right from the start'.

It was in the boiler room—the most vital part of the ship—that the main damage was done. This compartment, being so large, quickly filled with water and caused the bulkheads to give way. Thus the water rapidly penetrated to the other boiler rooms.

As Stoker Farnden scrambled up on deck the order 'Abandon ship' was being passed by word of mouth. The order had been piped at first, but no one heard it in the gale, so eventually the bosun's mate gave up the struggle. Now as the fateful words were passed from man to man they had a sobering effect. The seriousness of their plight slowly dawned on the men and instinct for discipline instilled over the years by countless drills and parades surged into their consciousness. The wild rush from below decks became an orderly procession to 'Abandon ship' stations.

The worst enemy of discipline was the howling gale. Most of the shouted orders went unheard amidst the devilish cacophony of the wind and the rolling roar of the waves.

*　　*　　*　　*　　*

Up on the bridge Captain Savill could hardly believe it had happened. The *Hampshire* mined in this position: it seemed incredible. He, too, was hampered by the noise of the gale, which made it impossible to ascertain quickly how serious the position was.

Almost by instinct he worked out in his head the ship's

position—slightly less than one and a half miles from shore, between the Brough of Birsay and Marwick Head. So near to safety, and yet so far in reality. He felt sure that the cruiser's plight would have been witnessed by observers ashore. There was a faint hope that destroyers might come to their assistance, but Captain Savill was under no illusions about their chances of rescue on a night like this.

Reports to the bridge soon made him aware that the cruiser could not last out much longer. Ten minutes, perhaps? Twenty at the most? Even that would be a lucky break. She was now well down by the head and heeling slightly to starboard. The best any of them could hope for was to keep afloat in boats and rafts until aid came.

Uppermost in the captain's mind was the problem of the safety of his illustrious passenger. Lord Kitchener had not stayed long at dinner; he had returned to his cabin to rest and read. The captain sent an officer to bring him up on deck.

Kitchener, however, had calmly left his cabin when the explosion occurred. Slowly and deliberately, with unfaltering steps, he went up the ladder and on to the quarter deck. Leading Seaman Rogerson described how he saw the Field-Marshal 'walking quite collectedly, talking to two of the officers. All three were wearing khaki but were without their greatcoats.'

Petty Officer Wesson saw him, too. Wesson had hurried to his boat station; he was in charge of the Carley raft stations on the starboard side.

'While I was waiting with the others,' said Wesson, 'an officer came with Lord Kitchener from the Captain's cabin.'

This was Lieutenant Matthews, the ship's Gunnery Officer. He called out, 'Make way for Lord Kitchener', and the men immediately cleared a passage to let the Field-Marshal pass.

Added Wesson: 'Lord Kitchener went on deck and I did not see him again after that. I won't say he didn't feel the strain of it all like the rest of us. But he gave no outward sign of nervousness. He just looked very ill. I am sure he was still aboard when I left the ship.'

H.M.S. *Hampshire* (*Photo*: Imperial War Museum)

Admiral Jellicoe bidding farewell to Lord Kitchener (*Photo*: Central Press)

A new and unexpected problem confronted the ship's company. It was impossible to launch the ship's boats mechanically, as the derricks were operated electrically and the current had failed.

One boat they did manage to lower by hand. The seamen in charge cut its lashings, and between fifty and sixty men leapt into it just before an enormous wave crashed over them. The boat, with its top-heavy cargo of humanity, was borne up on the crest of the wave high above the sinking ship. The next moment it was sucked down into the trough and broke in splintering fragments against the *Hampshire*'s side. A score of men were killed by the impact, crushed to death against the armour plating; the others were hurled into the swirling flotsam of planks and broken oars.

Impassively, the War Minister watched this disaster. He was gravely composed, speaking in monosyllables to Fitzgerald and Macpherson, who were by his side. As the *Hampshire* lurched still farther to starboard, he abruptly turned his back on the men working on the boats and rafts.

Captain Savill was helping his boat's crew to clear away the galley, evidently intending to get Kitchener into this boat. Leading Seaman Charles Rogerson heard the Captain call out to the Field-Marshal to come to the boat. 'But owing to noise made by wind and sea, I don't think Lord Kitchener could hear him.'

Even if he had heard, it could have made little difference. There never was any real chance of getting the boat safely launched. Perhaps Lord Kitchener realised this, and deliberately turned a deaf ear to the Captain's shouts. For a man of Kitchener's temperament there would have been something repellent about joining in an undignified rush to save his own skin, however highly his countrymen might value it. And, however much such an operation might have been disguised, however willingly the ship's company would have seen him to safety, all who knew Kitchener agreed that it would have been out of character for the man to have acted in this way.

L.K.D.—C

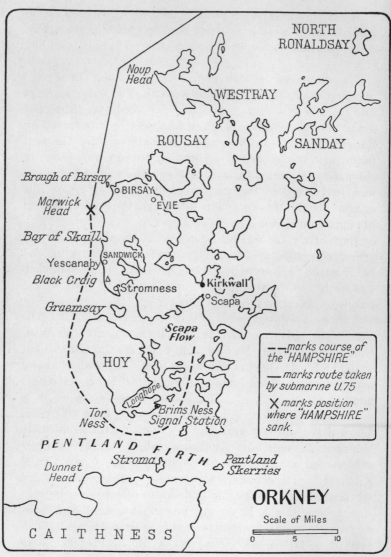

H.M.S. *Hampshire*'s route from Scapa Flow

Besides, the War Minister had often jokingly told his friends: 'My death has got to be by water.' It was a grimly fatalistic reference to the one occasion when he had his fortune read, and was told he would 'die on the water'.

Thus Kitchener never really had a chance. It is futile to argue that Captain Savill should not have wasted precious moments by trying to clear away his own boat, that instead he should have seen Kitchener safely into a raft. It is very doubtful whether Kitchener would have agreed to embark in a raft, and even more unlikely that he could have survived the ordeal.

Colonel Sir Henry Creedy, who was one of the War Minister's secretaries at the War Office, has testified that Kitchener keenly felt the cold of British winters after so many years in the East. 'Foreign climates have spoiled me,' said Kitchener, shivering, as each winter's morning, on arriving at the War Office, he ordered the fires to be stoked up again. 'He would never have survived in such icy water in such a gale,' said Sir Henry.

Meanwhile men were jumping overboard from the quarter-deck in their lifebelts and cork waistcoats. Others were washed off the decks by the sheer force of the waves. All around the doomed vessel men could be seen grabbing frantically at any piece of wreckage that came their way, holding on grimly. Many had been badly injured when the ship was hit; some were scalded when the boiler burst after the explosion. For these the salt water was like the lacerations of a razor.

Only eight minutes had passed since the explosion, but already it was obvious that the ship was sinking fast, and couldn't keep afloat much longer. Clouds of steam poured out of the foremost engine room on the starboard side.

Chief Shipwright Phillips did not even have a lifebelt. It was stowed away in his locker. 'I expect if I had had my lifebelt on, I should have acted differently and probably lost my life. But I could see that when the ship sank, the picket boat to which I was allotted would be entangled in our main rigging and go down with it.'

Phillips decided to stay aboard until he found a more hopeful way of leaving the ship.

Anything that would float was thrown overboard. Phillips and two others threw over their carpenter's bench, meaning to jump after it, but it was swept back against the ship and smashed into pieces. Two officers jumped overboard with cabin drawers under each arm.

Leading Seaman Rogerson permitted himself one last jest: 'What do they think they're doing?' he asked another seaman. 'Committing hara-kiri?'

Rogerson claimed he was the last man to remember seeing Kitchener. 'He was still on the quarter-deck, with his back to the bridge. I do not think he got into a boat. When I sprang on to a raft he was still on the starboard side of the quarter-deck, talking with his officers. From the time that elapsed between my leaving the ship and her sinking, I feel certain that Lord Kitchener went down with her and was on deck at the time she sank. Of the civilian members of his party I saw nothing.'

Abandoning all further attempts to launch the boats, the crew concentrated on getting away the Carley rafts. These huge oval lifeboats were 10 feet long and 8 feet wide, with a depth of 3 feet. Their edges were encircled by a structure of cork 1½ feet in diameter. To the floats were fitted gratings on which men stood or squatted, waist deep in water; the weight of fifty or more men pushed the raft deep in the sea.

Stoker Farnden helped to get away rafts numbers one and two, then himself took up position in number three. With a frantic heave he and his shipmates shoved off from the ship and paddled feverishly to get away. Already the *Hampshire*'s bows were dipping into the sea.

Wesson had been busy helping to open the hatches. As each one was heaved up men swarmed out from below. When he had finished this job he went back to his raft station. He was at number one raft and remained there until the water came up to the ridge rope.

Wesson cut the lashings of his raft and had it ready for launching. As he did so there was a rush of men, threatening to swamp the float. Fifty men managed to crowd on to it, probably twenty more jumped and missed. 'As we drew away from the ship several more injured men leaped on to the raft, knocking us over. I shall never forget the agonised screams as the salt water lashed their wounds,' said Wesson.

Furiously, but in orderly fashion, the men under Wesson managed somehow to paddle clear from the suction of the sinking vessel. In what seemed an age they were twenty yards from the *Hampshire*; each wave threatened to dash them back into the ship's side. A minute passed . . . a wave fortunately swept them farther away . . . fifty yards. Waist deep in foaming surf, they tossed like matchwood on the raging seas. Several were borne off the raft by the fury of the waves.

As the ship's funnel went under, Chief Shipwright Phillips decided he could not risk staying any longer. He had found nothing else to improvise as a raft since his carpenter's bench had been splintered to pieces. 'This is it,' he thought, as he kicked off his boots and jumped into the chill waters in a momentary lull between waves.

Phillips had timed his jump well. The lull probably didn't last more than twenty seconds, but it was long enough for him to strike out vigorously and swim clear of the ship. As he rose on the crest of the next wave he heard a muffled explosion, which he thought was the bursting of another boiler. At the same time he sighted a Carley raft about fifty yards away, and decided to make for this.

Few men could have had less chance of survival that June night than Chief Shipwright Phillips. No lifebelt, nothing to cling on to, an ice-cold sea that threatened cramp and fifty yards to travel—in a storm like this, the equivalent of a quarter of a mile in calm water.

But he made it. The effort of reaching the raft was almost too much for him. He was submerged under the float and hit his head on the heavy grating. In another moment he would have been drowned, but two men on the raft reached over and pulled him in.

Many men still aboard the *Hampshire* were convinced that it was safest to stay in the boats until the last possible moment, thinking that as the ship went under the boats would float away. Experience should have warned them against such a fallacy. At whatever angle the ship sank, the suction would inevitably draw them under. Probably many felt it was a choice of two deaths—either the slow, torturing death of a buffeting on a raft, or the more frightening but infinitely quicker end by sinking with the vessel.

Rogerson got away just in time. As he scrambled on to a raft he watched the last death throes of the cruiser. With a violent shudder and a dreadful grinding noise, she lurched forward and stood poised, propellers out of the water. Wesson, aboard his raft some hundred yards away, noticed the outline of the tilted boats and the derricks, with men still clinging on. 'It's suicide,' he thought. 'They'll die like rats in a trap. Nothing can save them.'

Men were still leaping off the quarter-deck, or sliding down the ship's side. Piercing screams told how they tore their bodies on the barnacles.

The evidence of the men on the rafts as to what happened to the men left behind was conflicting. One man claimed he saw the captain's galley slung on the third cutter's davits on the port side, but he was sure Kitchener did not get into it. Another said he saw the galley turned out, while a third insisted the galley was lowered. But on one point there was unanimity: no boats were seen to get away from the ship.

'She's going any moment,' hoarsely shouted a man in Wesson's raft. He was so shocked at the spectacle that he lurched forward, retched and slid off the float into the sea.

Then the *Hampshire* tucked her bows deeper into the water. Like a giant porpoise indolently somersaulting, she rolled over. Wesson closed his eyes. The rigging splintered and crashed, the boats, with the men still sitting in them, were dragged remorsely down. Like wooden puppets, their bodies toppled limply forward as the cruiser turned over. As Phillips had feared, the boats were inextricably caught up in the wrecked rigging. Scores of men must have lost their lives in this way.

There was a sickening gurgle, and within fifteen minutes of the explosion the *Hampshire* had plunged to the bottom.

3

'It's a Long Way to
Scapa Flow-Oh-o!'

THERE was nothing on the sea within the radius of the horizon when the *Hampshire* went down. This fact alone made a heavy loss of life certain.

Even so, many more lives could have been saved but for a combination of ill luck, dilatoriness, stupidity and incompetence. It is not known what attempts, if any, Captain Savill made to inform the authorities ashore of what had happened. No officers from the cruiser survived to testify whether he did, or did not, take action to pass a signal. It might have been that his verbal instructions were lost in the gale and never carried out. Even if wireless communication was impossible because of the failure of the electric power, visual signals could have been made. Nobody ashore saw any such signals, nor did they observe any distress rockets.

Possibly Captain Savill felt sure that the ship's plight must have been seen from the shore. In this he was right, but civilian observers admitted afterwards that, had they seen rockets fired, they would probably have acted more promptly.

Mr. McKay, a crofter, said: 'I thought I heard a noise like an explosion, but in a gale like that one couldn't be certain. It might have been gunfire, or it might have been thunder. In any case in a sea riding as high as this, it wasn't easy to decide whether the ship was in difficulty or not.

'I remember waiting to see whether there would be any

distress signals. There weren't, so I paid no more attention.'

Even if one accepts the Admiralty version: '. . . the electric power failed . . . and no wireless communication was possible', one would nevertheless have thought that the *Hampshire* would have had battery-operated, emergency transmission apparatus, as did other cruisers in World War I. None of the survivors is sure about this; two thought the cruiser carried no auxiliary wireless, another was certain that she did. The remainder thought that the order 'Abandon ship' was given so promptly that there was no time to send a wireless message. But between ten and fifteen minutes is, by naval standards, sufficient time for emergency measures to have been taken, and in the case of the *Hampshire*, if the ship had auxiliary wireless, it would have been a grave dereliction of duty for the captain not to have ordered its use.

It was a gloomy evening, the sky was overcast with scudding, black clouds and there was a driving mist of rain. But, though visibility was not good, it was still daylight. Darkness, in fact, does not fall until about 11 p.m. in the month of June in this latitude.

Joe Angus was a gunner in the Orkney Territorial Forces and on that fatal night he was on duty at the look-out post at Birsay, manned by a non-commissioned officer and men of the Orkney Royal Garrison Artillery. He watched the cruiser as she appeared out of the mist and was somewhat surprised she was so close inshore.

'I hadn't been looking very long when all of a sudden a cloud of smoke and flame burst up from behind the bridge. She suddenly changed course and was steaming in for the land. The cruiser was passing Marwick Head when the explosion occurred and she gradually sank down by the bow.'

The 'change of course' to which he refers was merely the ship, out of control, swinging off course while she still had way on. It was not, as some ashore thought, an attempt by Captain Savill to beach her in shallow water.

Joe Angus estimated that the ship sank in 'about fifteen

minutes'. He was positive that he saw no distress signals. Though he saw the explosion, he heard nothing: the strong wind must have deadened the sound.

Doubtless this is the reason why so few people witnessed the disaster. It also explains why the few who saw it did not realise the seriousness of the situation—like crofter McKay, who went away before the ship sank.

Joe Angus was the first person to give the alarm. He raced to his billet close by and reported to Corporal Drever, from Sandy Island, the man in charge, that a ship was in distress.

There were only three men at this look-out post and Drever immediately hurried to the post office, 200 yards away, to give the news. Joe Angus, who is still alive, thinks the report was passed by telephone to Kirkwall and to Naval Headquarters at Longhope, but the Admiralty stated afterwards that there was no telephone at Birsay and that any message must have been passed by telegraph. At any rate there is ample confirmation from all sources that the alarm must have been given shortly after 8 p.m.

One report afterwards stated that 'the N.C.O. in charge of the Birsay patrol, Corporal Mowat, tried to telephone the Vice-Admiral in command of the Longhope station'. There is no evidence that 'Corporal Mowat' ever existed. No one has ever heard of him and, as far as is known, Corporal Drever was the only N.C.O. present and the only man to give the alarm.

Meanwhile the sub-postmistress at Birsay had herself seen the ship sinking and, anticipating that a telegraph message would have to be sent, rushed back to the post office to have a form ready. Corporal Drever could not have lost any time in reaching the post office because it is clear from the message he drafted out that he had not waited to see the ship sink.

The pencilled message read: 'Battle cruiser seems in distress between Marwick Head and the Brough of Birsay.' According to Admiralty sources this message was addressed in duplicate to the Commander, Western Patrol, Stromness and to 'Artillery' (the telegraphic address of the Commanding Officer of the

R.G.A., Kirkwall). It was timed as being handed in at 8.45 British Summer Time—i.e. 7.45 G.M.T.

In fact it seems probable that the time given was wrong, that it should have been at least ten and possibly fifteen or twenty, minutes later. While one cannot fix the time of the explosion with certainty, it must have been very close to 8 p.m. G.M.T., and that was the hour when Joe Angus went on duty. If the explosion occurred before 8 p.m., then he must have taken up his look-out a few minutes early.

The Admiralty stated afterwards, 'It should be explained that at the time of sending the message the corporal was un-aware that an explosion had occurred, though it is impossible to say whether in the excitement of the moment the gunner on duty did not mention the fact, or whether the corporal did not grasp what was told him.'

This is unfair to both. Joe Angus could not hear the ex-plosion in the gale; therefore, the corporal would not be aware of it either. However, as he was returning to the look-out, the *Hampshire* disappeared beneath the waves before Drever's startled gaze. Realising now the gravity of the situation, he lost no time in returning to the post office. But by that time the message had been transmitted to Kirkwall.

Both the postmistress and Drever were in a state of agitation and probably in their desire to put matters right speedily they only added to the confusion.

'The ship has sunk. Can that be added to the message?' asked Drever.

'Oh, dear,' replied the postmistress, visibly aghast at the tidings, 'the message has gone through now. I'd better let them know what has happened.'

Both of them believed that the ship which had sunk was a battle cruiser. That had been Drever's inaccurate description, and though the postmistress was not well versed in naval matters, she realised that a battle cruiser was a very big ship.

So perhaps the panic was understandable. Instead of draft-ing a message which corrected the original, the postmistress merely signalled to Kirkwall: 'The ship has sunk. Can that be added to the telegram?'

There was a brief pause. Then came a curt reply that 'it was all right'. Corporal Drever seemed a bit dubious that it was, but the postmistress assured him that Kirkwall had understood her. The fatal error was that no new signal was dispatched, nor was any formal correction to the original made. In fact, the additional information that the ship had sunk was not even written on a telegraph form. Documentary evidence of their undoubted intention to add to the original telegram was therefore lacking.

Though there might be some excuse for the harassed pair in Birsay Post Office, there was surely none for the two telegraphists at Kirkwall. They received the additional message from the postmistress that the ship had sunk, but, probably because it was informally worded, did not add this important information to the original telegram. Technically, they may have been correct, but their omission and, above all, their failure to query back, showed a lamentable lack of initiative and commonsense. It should have dawned on them that a major catastrophe had occurred. Indeed, as far as they were concerned, a worse catastrophe than in fact it was, for the original message mentioned a battle cruiser, not a cruiser.

The first telegraphist passed the original message to his colleague, who took the copy for the Commander, Western Patrol, Stromness, and passed it on. While he was sending this dispatch, the first telegraphist wrote the copy for the R.G.A. He admitted at the inquiry that he had heard from the operator that the ship had sunk, but he did not understand that he was being asked to add that information to the original telegram.

Thus it was not until 8.20 p.m. that, owing to some misgivings on the part of the postmistress at Birsay, a second telegram consisting of the words 'vessel down' was dispatched to Stromness, where it was received at 8.31 p.m. This was followed by a third message at 8.35 p.m. stating that 'Four-funnel cruiser sunk twenty minutes ago. No assistance arrived yet.

Send ships to pick up bodies.' This was received in Stromness at 8.50 p.m.

Meanwhile the original message was being scanned with mixed feelings of incredulity and cynicism. Far from alerting the authorities, it only seemed to irritate them. After a delay of several minutes, back came a query from Stromness asking what class of ship was in distress.

Years later, the Admiralty placidly commented: 'The mention of a battle cruiser did not conclusively identify the ship with the *Hampshire* which was, of course, not a battle cruiser.'

Perhaps not. Yet the Vice-Admiral at Longhope, Vice-Admiral Sir F. E. Brock, had been one of the small party of flag officers who had met Lord Kitchener at lunch in the *Iron Duke*, and therefore knew of his departure aboard the *Hampshire*.

One of the Orkney Territorials later tried to telephone the Vice-Admiral when he realised that the naval signal station did not appreciate the situation and was wasting time by ridiculous procedure. He was told that the Vice-Admiral had left instructions that he was not to be disturbed! Unabashed, and determined to break through this barrier of non-co-operation, he then telephoned the Senior Naval Officer at Stromness, who had a number of ships available. These could have been put to sea immediately and quickly reached the scene of disaster.

But the Senior Naval Officer replied: 'I cannot order any ships to sea. I have had no official information of what you say has happened, and I cannot take the responsibility for sending ships to the rescue until I have received instructions from the Vice-Admiral at Longhope.'

In disgust the Territorial gave up trying to do anything on his own initiative. He decided that no one would listen to a mere private soldier.

Thus valuable time was lost. Meanwhile many men died.

* * * * *

There was no room for all on the few Carley rafts which were launched from the cruiser. As far as is known only three rafts got safely away, each with a load of anything from fifty to seventy men. But on the raft which originally carried the seventy men, only six survived. Every raft was loaded up well beyond the safety limit, for while two of these floats could have taken forty-five men as a maximum load in normal conditions, the third float was only designed to carry eighteen. As a result men were standing in icy water nearly up to their chests. while others were hanging on to the ratlines over the side as long as their strength held out.

Many men threshed about them wildly in the water until they were so buffeted and stunned by the waves that they either lost consciousness or gave up the fight and died. These were the men who relied on their lifebelts and cork waistcoats. Many more must have been sucked down into the sea by the vortex caused by the sinking vessel.

Probably 200 men either squatted on the rafts or held on to pieces of wreckage in those first ten minutes after the ship went down. Of these, about fifty must have died within a quarter of an hour. Some were tossed off the rafts by the force of the elements; and then, the freezing water slowly sapped their energy until they could hold on no longer. The ratlines cut into their hands, tore off the skin; gradually numbed fingers lost their grip. Others were half clad and died of exposure.

On Stoker Farnden's raft about fifty men gathered, but one by one they disappeared. 'All around us,' said Farnden, 'there were floating bodies. Other men were clinging to lifebelts and pieces of wreckage and calling for help. But it was impossible to rescue them.'

The small float capsized twice and its complement was soon reduced to six. In such a sea it was quite impossible to guide the rafts, which were driven past Marwick Head before the violent N.N.W. wind and the strong tide. According to the records of the Deerness anemometer, the storm was at its height at the time the *Hampshire* sank.

The raft on which Phillips found himself was submerged by the weight of seventy men. It was generally agreed that if they continued like this nobody would survive. So, without any argument, and almost by a process of subconscious reasoning, it was decided to lighten the raft by asking for volunteers from among those wearing lifebelts to leave the float.

The Royal Navy is always at its best in moments like this. A dozen men cheerfully agreed to jump off the raft and keep afloat as best they could. With a touch of bravado and jokes about 'We'll get to shore first anyhow', and 'See you back in Scapa', they plunged into the sea. Their example prompted another six to follow suit.

'This eased the floating capacity of the raft,' said Phillips, 'but those of us still aboard it were standing in four feet of water, and it was tough luck on the little 'uns. Often their heads went right under.'

Standing next to Phillips was a soldier, one of the officers' servants on Lord Kitchener's staff.

'Shall we reach the shore?' he inquired anxiously.

'I think we'll do it,' replied Phillips, more to console the soldier than to express his real opinion.

The soldier shook his head hopelessly. 'I don't think so, mate,' he mumbled.

He had barely uttered these words than his head sagged backwards, with his mouth wide open. 'I was sure he was dead,' said Phillips. 'He was rigid and eventually he slipped to the bottom of the raft.'

Yet now, only a mile away, was the grimly forbidding Orkney coastline, jagged and crater-like on the sky-line. That was the irony of it all.

Old Tom Jennings, a grey and grizzled gunner, tried to raise the men's spirits with a song. But even this tough old salt could only manage an emaciated, crow-like crackle as he roared against the wind:

> 'It's a long way to Tipperary,
> It's a long, long way to go ...
> It's a long way from Scapa ...
> From Scapa Flow-oh-o!'

Gunner Jennings' eyes were glazed and bloodshot as he bellowed out the words with pathetically feigned gaiety, using up all his strength. But, though some joined in the chorus, they eventually gave up singing and decided to conserve their energies. Jennings, however, refused to be silenced either by his shipmates or the elements. Upbraiding those who had ceased to join in his choruses, he tried to stand up and conduct them. It was a foolish error for an old seaman: as the next big wave closed over the raft Jennings slipped. When the wave had passed he was not in sight.

One of the bravest that June night was a lad of seventeen, the smallest in the whole ship's company. He could hardly keep his chin above water in the swamped raft, but he gripped the arms of a taller man and, in between the spells of buffeting, sang snatches of various popular numbers. But the effort of singing was too much for him, too, and finally, sinking to the bottom of the raft, he died.

What happened to the officers remains a mystery. Some saw Captain C. S. Hazeon, Royal Marines, swim to a raft and then leave it when he saw how crowded it was. Others saw Lieutenant-Commander F. G. Stewart clinging to some wreckage for quite a time after the ship sank. The chaplain, the Reverend P. G. Alexander, stayed aboard to the last to comfort those who sat waiting in the boats. Many officers must have been sucked down with the ship.

Leading Seaman Rogerson was numbed as he held on grimly to his float. An overpowering desire to sleep came over him. 'To get over this we thumped each other on the back, for no man who went to sleep ever woke again. When men died it was just as though they were falling asleep.

'I got them singing, but they still kept dropping off the raft. They were clustered round you, dying as you looked at them. They were people of fine physique, yet it made no difference.'

It was one of the coldest June nights for years. As the minutes ticked away the realisation grew that no help was

A contemporary artist's impression of the sinking of H.M.S. *Hampshire* (*Courtesy of* Illustrated Newspapers)

Site where survivors landed (*Photo:* T. Kent, Kirkwall)

Stoker Walter Farnden, a survivor
(*Photo: Radio Times*, Hulton Picture Library)

within sight and that even if it came, rescue work would be hazardous in the extreme.

One man started to sing 'Pack up your troubles in your old kitbag', and ended up by chattering a lot of incomprehensible gibberish. A few lost their reason in the ordeal of the storm. Some had no will to live and succumbed without a fight, just rolling off into the sea to end the agony. Others were so eager to survive that they struggled too hard and had no reserve strength to fall back on.

It was force of character more than physique that enabled the few to carry on. Character that provided the will-power and discipline to relax in the occasional lulls and brace themselves when the next big wave came. Character that withstood the agonies of suffering and death all around them. And these few men, who stood it better than the rest, knew they were in no position to help their less fortunate comrades, for if they once let go their hold to rescue a fallen shipmate, they would be pitched off the raft.

One man in Rogerson's raft stood upright for five hours with dead men lying all around him. It seemed a miracle that he held on at all, with his bleeding wrists wedged in the ropes. Another died in Rogerson's arms.

An hour passed, then two. By this time forty-three men had died on Wesson's raft. The four who were left had passed a score of floating bodies, horribly mangled. Occasionally they had seen men shrieking to be dragged aboard, but it was impossible to attempt rescue. The storm did not permit of any heroism. A few—a very few—still had some life left in them and were clinging to lifebelts and planks, but all fight had been knocked out of them by the elements.

Three hours passed. It was light until about 11 p.m., but now dusk began to envelop the scene and blot out the sight of land. And still there was no sign of any rescue craft. As night fell, most of the survivors had given up hope.

Rogerson reckoned he had spent five hours in his raft. Probably it seemed longer than it was. 'As we got near land, the situation grew worse,' he said. 'The wind was blowing on shore and many must have been dashed against the rocks and killed.'

With a crunching jolt one of the rafts struck a submerged rock, flinging two men to their death on the barnacle-covered crags.

At many places along this stretch of coast the line of sheer cliff is broken by deep, narrow gaps running inland for some distance, where the sea has eroded flaws in the rocks. All along these gaps lie small boulders broken up by innumerable gales, and the Orcadians testify how, in a violent storm, the sea will toss these boulders for yards, breaking them up into still smaller fragments. Such gaps in the cliff are known locally as 'geos'. It was into the geos that the rafts were driven.

Both Farnden and Wesson found themselves in a geo. 'It was just a small inlet, not more than twelve feet wide. And I could not swim,' said Farnden. 'But somehow I made it, though whether I waded through it, or how I managed it, I do not know.

'I just felt firm land beneath me and knew I was saved. I held on to the rock, breathless.'

Phillips noticed that the gulls had already spotted the men on the rafts and were hovering around, in the twilight, wailing. 'Wailing and waiting like vultures until all signs of life had gone. How I loathed those gulls at that moment.'

His arms and legs were completely numbed, his voice had gone and now the fatal, creeping death of sleepiness was coming over him. He was lying across dead bodies with his hands jammed between the rope bindings of the raft and his head resting on its side.

'But my mind was normal. I remember thinking that perhaps twenty of us were still alive. Then at last one huge wave bore us against a very high cliff only to drop us down in a trough again out of reach of the shore.

'I am certain that, had I possessed more strength at the time, I should have dropped over the side and ended it all.'

Maybe it was lack of strength, or perhaps Phillips had more of the instinct for survival than he knew. But somehow he clung on, waiting for the next wave. This time, by a stroke of luck, the raft was swept clear of the high cliff and caught up on some low rocks in the geo. This saved the lives of the six survivors on that raft, ejecting them together with the dead bodies on to the shore.

Meanwhile Wesson had secured a precarious foothold at the bottom of a sheer precipice. There seemed no hope of climbing this in the dark, even if he had had the strength. Yet he dared not stay where he was; to do so courted being swept back into the raging sea. Each time he and his companions tried to struggle up and grope for a nook in which to shelter, they were sucked back by the waves and flung on to the rocks with the next breaker, bleeding and dazed.

'The sea had drawn the raft away,' said Wesson. 'I was left alone with waves hurtling over me. I never thought I could make it under such a terrific battering.

'But each time a wave broke I scrambled a little farther up the cliff-side. I was numb with cold. My limbs felt like lead and my hands were mangled. Salt water on my lacerated flesh was like red-hot needles.'

Rogerson did not remember how he got ashore. 'All feeling had gone out of me and I don't know what happened once we touched the rocks. But I remember when I was picked up, the people said it was the worst storm they had had in Orkney for years.'

Farnden and Wesson plodded on separately. Somehow they both managed to clamber up the rock face, which, in the geo, was less precipitous. Wesson, his legs almost as useless as lead weights, struggled on, hand over hand, inch by inch over the towering boulders. Sometimes he felt he must slip back out of sheer exhaustion. He reckoned afterwards that his climb must have taken him an hour with frequent breaks while he paused for breath. Then, gradually, the rock face became less steep. For a minute he lay panting and longed to stay where he was and fall asleep. Very nearly he succumbed to this temptation, but, as his hand groped out, he felt the flat surface only a foot above him. He was at the top.

When he drew himself over the last rock the effort proved too much for him. This time he had not the will power to combat sleepiness any longer. He sank to the ground and buried his face in the wet grass . . . perhaps for half an hour, perhaps only for five minutes. By then he had lost count or sense of time. When he opened his eyes again, he noticed a light just ahead of him. He tried to struggle to his feet, but could not. Edging himself along on his stomach, he crawled slowly towards the friendly glimmer. It was just a faint light from the window of a crofter's cottage. Lying on his back, he had just enough strength left to kick on the door with his foot. When the door opened, he collapsed and lost consciousness.

4

'If You Launch the Lifeboat, It's Mutiny'

ORCADIANS are still loath to talk about the happenings of that night of June 5. This may be native reticence, or even shyness at revealing the help they so unstintingly offered, for the Orcadians are a naturally modest people. But one has the indelible impression that the tragedy of the *Hampshire* was one from which they have never quite recovered.

As one of them put it to me: 'It was not so much that lives were lost, but that we were stopped from saving more of these poor men. That is what we can never forget and never forgive.'

Whom do they never forgive? They will say little more than, 'it was the fault of officialdom'. Not only at the time of the disaster, but for many years afterwards, some of them were threatened with penalties if they talked about the events of that searing night. 'Officialdom' did not hesitate to invoke war-time regulations when it came to silencing the Orcadians. As this narrative will subsequently reveal, the people of these islands were often treated as though they themselves might have been the enemy, such was the zeal of the authorities to keep the whole incident an 'official secret'.

Very few people who were eye-witnesses of these events are still alive. One lady now living in Birsay was a child at the time and, though she declines to have her name published, has written a brief account of what happened that night.

'My mother used to tell me of that evening. My nephew,

who was then a little boy, came running in to tell my mother that there was a ship off Marwick Head "sending up a queer reek".

'It was after school-time and my sister ran out to see what was happening. A column of steam and spray stood up into the air; the vessel turned, as if she were making for the shore, but in a matter of seconds she stood bows up and just disappeared.

'My sister, instead of taking her bicycle, went on foot to Birsay Post Office (then kept by Miss Jessie Comloquoy) to ask her to send a message to the naval authorities in Kirkwall. While she was delivering the message, a Mr. Robertson from Quatquoy, Marwick, came in.

'He had ridden on horseback down over the Links to send a message. Then a Territorial, one of those stationed at Marwick Head, arrived and my sister and Mr. Robertson "handed over" to him.'

As far as can be ascertained, only Mr. Robertson, Corporal Drever, Joe Angus, Miss Comloquoy and the young girl and little boy already mentioned actually saw the disaster and realised what happened. Crofter McKay thought the ship was all right because he saw no distress signals, and turned away before she sank.

When the message about a 'battle-cruiser in distress' was received at Stromness, the first action of the Commander, Western Patrol, the late Captain (at that time Commander) D. M. Walker, R.N., was to order the yacht *Jason II* and the trawler *Cambodia* to be ready to put to sea at once. He then telephoned the Vice-Admiral at Longhope, read him the telegram and asked whether he should dispatch the two vessels.

Vice-Admiral Brock did not know that the *Hampshire* had taken the western route, though he certainly should have been notified. He merely asked for further details and suggested no action should be taken until further information was obtained. He did however take the precaution of telephoning to Brims Ness Signal Station, at the south-east extremity of Hoy, to inquire what ship had passed to the westward and at what time.

He was promptly informed that the *Hampshire* had passed there at 6.45 p.m. B.S.T.

The Admiralty have not published details of the telegram requesting more information. But independent evidence suggests that Birsay Post Office was only asked to state what class of vessel was in trouble and that no request was made for the ship's position when she sank. In any case, to confuse the issue, this telegram crossed with the message stating 'vessel down'. The captain of *Jason II* and the skipper of *Cambodia* were in Commander Walker's office when the latter message was received at 9.37 p.m. and they sailed immediately, not knowing the identity of the ship to whose rescue they were proceeding.

In the White Paper *Cmd* 2710, published by the Admiralty in June, 1926, on 'The Loss of H.M.S. *Hampshire*', it was stated: 'It is quite untrue to say that no adequate rescue operations were attempted at sea until the following day.' I have found no documentary evidence that anyone made such an allegation.

The White Paper stated further that: 'There has been criticism from some quarters because the Stromness 40-foot auxiliary motor-lifeboat was not called out. (Another version, that the lifeboat was *not allowed* by the Commander, Western Patrol, to put out, can be definitely contradicted on contemporary evidence.)

'As Captain Walker is dead, it is not possible to obtain first-hand information as to his reasons for not calling upon the motor-lifeboat. In all probability, however, he was of the opinion, firstly that he had ample Naval vessels available for rescue work—as was undoubtedly the case—and secondly, that the motor-lifeboat would not be able to face the sea conditions then existing.

'On this latter point, the only valuable evidence is that of the men who were actually at sea that night and experienced the real conditions. Their evidence, so far as is known to the

Admiralty, is unanimous that the lifeboat could never have reached the spot except under tow.'

This statement is unsatisfactory because the Admiralty quoted no sources for its 'contemporary evidence'. All the contemporary evidence now available refutes their arguments; all Orcadians still living who have first-hand knowledge of that night are unanimous in agreeing that the Naval authorities prevented the lifeboat from being launched. Their attitude is summed up in the words of Joe Angus, now a Stromness grocer, who says: 'Far more lives could have been saved if things had been conducted in a commonsense way, but red tape has been the death of many a poor fellow.'

Years afterwards a statement was made that the lifeboat 'put to sea five hours after the explosion occurred, only to be recalled by the Naval authorities after it had covered three miles towards the cruiser'.

This is not so. The records of the Stromness branch of the Royal National Lifeboat Institution show that the lifeboat was not launched between 17 December 1914, and 27 January 1920.

News of the disaster reached the lifeboatmen about the same time that the first signal was passed to Stromness. There is no positive evidence of how they heard, but everyone seems agreed that the information did not come from the Naval authorities, as one would have expected. Indeed, when the latter heard that Mr. George Linklater Thomson, honorary secretary of the Stromness R.N.L.I. branch, knew about a cruiser being in distress, they gave the impression of being extremely irritated.

Mr. Thomson was a man highly respected in the neighbourhood and his evidence on this subject can be regarded as reliable, fearless and uncompromising. He had been secretary of the branch for many years and was one of the most knowledgeable men in the district on matters of seamanship. The Royal National Lifeboat Institution held him in great esteem and appointed him a Life Governor of the Institution, which is the highest honour that can be bestowed by them on an honorary worker. He was also a Justice of the Peace.

When he heard about the sinking of a vessel off Marwick Head, he telephoned to Stromness Naval H.Q. to ask for confirmation. He was told peremptorily: 'We cannot discuss the movements of warships.'

'But,' insisted Mr. Thomson, 'I am not asking about their movements. I understand from a reliable source that a cruiser is in distress and I should like to offer the services of the lifeboat.'

'We know nothing about a cruiser,' he was told, and the voice at the other end rang off.

Meanwhile orders were given for the lifeboat to be prepared for sea. She was a well appointed lifeboat with motor power and manned by a crew of local fishermen who knew the area around Marwick Head intimately and had long experience of the vagaries of the strong currents in the vicinity. The crew were standing by in their lifebelts when Mr. Thomson decided that he ought to make a personal call at Naval Headquarters.

On Mr. Thomson's personal testimony—and this has been confirmed by Mr. J. G. Sinclair, of Stromness, who is still alive —he offered to send the lifeboat out and his offer was 'bluntly and rudely declined'.

Feeling that he must press his case to a senior officer, Mr. Thomson insisted on seeing Captain Walker personally. This officer not only refused point-blank to allow the lifeboat to be launched, but worked himself up into a fury on the subject.

'You have no right to interfere in Naval matters. It is none of your bloody business,' he stormed. 'And, what's more, if you attempt to launch the lifeboat, it's mutiny. Mutiny, do you hear? Any more nonsense or argument and I'll have the whole lot of you locked up.'

The events of that night had evidently been too much for Captain Walker. But Mr. Thomson was deeply hurt and bewildered at the reception he was given. 'He met with the utmost discourtesy, some say abuse, from the authorities, and the matter rankled in his mind until the day of his death,' said Mr. J. G. Sinclair.

'We had been out in seas just as bad before this,' was Mr. Thomson's wry comment, 'yet on the one occasion in the war when we could have done a worthwhile job, we were stopped.'

Orcadians describe the Admiralty's alibi that the lifeboat could not have been of any assistance that night as 'absolute nonsense'. Mr. Sinclair says that 'everyone connected with the lifeboat service in Stromness knows that many more lives could have been saved if Mr. Thomson's offer had been accepted.'

The lifeboat could have been launched an hour and a half before any other ship put out to the rescue. Thus was valuable time lost. It was not until 9.45 p.m. that Captain Walker, after a telephone talk with the Vice-Admiral, put to sea in the ocean-going tug, *Flying Kestrel*, with the trawlers, *Northward* and *Renzo*. The Vice-Admiral then ordered 'every available vessel' to put to sea, yet those under his command still declined to include the lifeboat in the rescue expedition. The lifeboatmen, who had willingly volunteered to go out and brave the gale, were puzzled and naturally resentful. Sometimes the excuse given was that 'they hadn't a chance'; other lifeboatmen were told it was 'a matter of security'.

In Orkney today there is still controversy about the times when the various naval craft went to the rescue. Some dispute the Admiralty's version and allege that no ships went out until three hours after the original message was sent. But it would seem that no warning signal was sent to the Commander-in-Chief, for the Admiralty stated later 'as soon as Vice-Admiral Brock received the news that the *Hampshire* had gone down, he immediately communicated it himself by telephone to the Commander-in-Chief.' But for a long time the Vice-Admiral had declined to admit even to himself that the *Hampshire* might have been involved.

The C.-in-C. ordered out four destroyers—*Owl*, *Midge* and, once again, *Unity* and *Victor*. The logs of *Unity* and *Victor* showed that they left between 10 p.m. and 10.10 p.m., 'steaming at 20 knots'. They may have been ordered to sail at this speed, but it is certain that no destroyer could have averaged more than 12 to 15 knots in such a gale. The Vice-Admiral also ordered the yacht *Zaza* and the trawler, *City of Selby*, then at the north of Orkney, to proceed southwards to the scene of the sinking. But it was not until 3.30 a.m. the following day that five other destroyers—*Munster*, *Menace*, *Napier*, *Oak* and *Opal* —went out 'to search for survivors'.

Weather reports at Stromness show that the storm did not abate until after midnight, that the N.N.W. wind was full gale force, with a 20-foot sea running and a strong incoming tide. Under such conditions the destroyers did well to overtake *Flying Kestrel* off Kirk Rocks and to catch up with *Jason II* and *Cambodia* just before the latter were off Marwick Head. This was somewhere 'between 10 and 10.30 (G.M.T.)', according to the Admiralty White Paper. But observers ashore were equally emphatic that it was after midnight (B.S.T.) before any vessel was sighted near where the cruiser sank.

Corporal Drever and Joe Angus were both positive that it was 'after midnight'. So was the crofter, Mr. McKay, and many other civilians ashore. On the other hand the Admiralty claimed that the signal log of H.M.S. *Unity* showed she encountered wreckage at 11.30 B.S.T., and that the ships 'made considerable use of their searchlights, not only over the sea, but on the coast, in the attempt to discover boats or rafts, and in the hope of assisting rescue parties ashore'.

'Our complaint was that we had no assistance from any craft at sea. I saw no searchlight before at least 1 p.m.,' declared Mr. McKay.

And the evidence of Farnden, Wesson and Phillips was that they saw no sign of rescue craft at any time.

*　　*　　*　　*　　*

The lack of co-operation between the Naval authorities and the Stromness lifeboat service was regrettable and inexplicable. The confusion over the telegraph messages was unfortunate,

but understandable. Delay in ordering all ships to the rescue
was also deplorable. But, in the circumstances, it must be admitted that rescue work from the sea would in all eventualities
have been severely handicapped.

Where the authorities blundered most was in their belated
attempts to organise rescue parties on land. This was the fatal
blunder which cost many lives, and for which there is no excuse
except stupidity.

The fact is that the Naval authorities at Stromness refused
to accept verbal assurances from civilians that a major warship
had sunk off Marwick Head and insisted they must wait for
confirmation. Mr. Thomson was very bitter about the 'chink-
ling of glasses of pink gin in an adjacent room while I put my
case to the Naval commander'. Nobody in Stromness Naval
circles could have known just how bad the weather was in the
vicinity of Marwick Head. Admiral Jellicoe wrote afterwards: 'In spite of the fact that the destroyers had been sent
back, it seemed almost incredible that the wind and sea could
have risen to such an extent as was actually the case, as the
conditions in Scapa Flow were not so bad as to indicate so extremely heavy a sea off the Brough of Birsay; and even when it
was reported that the *Hampshire* had sunk, there was reason
to hope that Lord Kitchener and his mission would be saved
by boat.'

And even when the awful facts eventually penetrated the
unwilling minds of those at Stromness, each waited for the
other to give an order. As for the 'adequate number of Naval
vessels' sent to the rescue, the truth is that not one of them
picked up a single survivor.

But, if little was done afloat until it was too late, even less
was done to effect rescue from the shore. Why was nothing
done to alert the crofters and to organise parties to search for
survivors and provide signal flares to lend hope to the men on
the rafts?

'Some of the crew must have perished trying to land on the
rocky coast after such long exposure, *and some died after*

landing,' stated the Admiralty. They died for the reason that there was no search party to assist them.

It may reasonably be asked why the few civilians ashore who saw the disaster did not pass the news on and organise rescue parties themselves. The answer is that they were prevented from doing so by the Naval and Military authorities—in some cases forcibly prevented under dire threats.

'There is no doubt that the actions of the Naval authorities on that night resulted in unnecessary loss of life. Local men, many of whom had an intimate knowledge of the cliffs in that area, were prevented from going near to render assistance. It would appear that the chief concern of the Navy was to keep the disaster secret for as long as possible,' is the view of Mr. J. G. Sinclair.

A raft, with nearly forty men on board, was washed into a geo northward of Skaill Bay, says Mr. John Folsetter. 'The cliffs were too high for them to scale and all were lost, but local people could have got them from the top with ropes, had they not been forbidden to go near the coast.'

The White Paper attempted, by implication, to pin some of the blame on the local Territorials by damning them with faint praise. 'The Vice-Admiral Commanding Orkneys and Shetlands, who made an investigation on the 12th June into the steps taken by the look-out at Birsay, reported to the Commander-in-Chief that, taking into consideration the fact that the Territorials who were there were not trained men, he considered that they did all that could be expected in the circumstances.'

It was not until just before he sailed with the rescue vessels that the Commander, Western Patrol, Stromness, telephoned to Lieutenant-Colonel Brooke, R.M.A., Fire Commander, Western Defences, Stromness, that a shore party would be required to search the north-west coast, and that motor-cars were being obtained for the purpose. Thus it was not until at least an hour and a quarter after the original message was received that any vehicle was available to go to Birsay.

Two cars were eventually found and a party, headed by Lieutenant Boissier, R.M.A., and a Naval surgeon named Pickup, set off with a sergeant and ten men. Unfortunately both Lieutenant Boissier and the Naval surgeon are dead, and their version of the night's events has not been told. Laden with ropes, blankets and lanterns, they set off. 'But,' said one of the Army privates afterwards, 'the lanterns were no use because the fuel had been left behind.'

This was not the only blunder. Not a single member of the party knew the district well, and when a civilian offered to come as guide, his services were abruptly declined. The Admiralty version is that the cars 'made for Marwick Head, in accordance with information received as to the scene of the accident (sic), but nearing there, were diverted to the south with the information that a neighbouring farmer had reported seeing four boats or rafts put off from the ship, and driven south'.

Civilians tell a very different story. On at least two occasions the drivers stopped to inquire the way; each time they were on the wrong road and had to be re-directed.

Now, if the Admiralty statement that they had been diverted to the south of Marwick Head were correct, one would have expected them to go to the area around Skaill Bay. The evidence of Mr. William Phillips, one of the Orcadians who went to the rescue on his own account, is that the cars arrived long after the survivors had come ashore and that 'they had come by way of Evie'.

'Why they had been to Evie, which is on the extreme northeast of the island, when Marwick Head was on the north-west, nobody could understand. I can only think they must have had no idea which way to take and so added an unnecessary fourteen miles to their journey.'

The Admiralty White Paper insisted that at about 10.8 p.m. the Vice-Admiral 'directed the Commander, Western Patrol, to take steps to warn all inhabitants along the coast to assist in any possible manner, and that a motor cyclist was dispatched within a short time for this purpose.' Such instructions may have been given by the Vice-Admiral, but the Commander, Western Patrol, was not there to carry them out, and not a single civilian recalls any such warning being given by a motor cyclist or anyone else.

Only very few people knew of the disaster in the vicinity of Birsay. They did not pass the news on to their neighbours for two reasons; first, they expected that the Naval and Military authorities would organise search parties, and, secondly, later on in the night, they were arbitrarily told to mind their own business and to talk to nobody about the affair.

Said one crofter: 'Mr. McKay told me the news very late that night. I went down the cliff path from my cottage to see what could be done, but I was told by a soldier that all civilians were to remain in their houses and not to venture near the shore or we should be fired on.'

This does not sound like warning the inhabitants 'to assist in any possible manner'.

Mr. William Phillips and his party of crofters were later ordered away from the shore by a Naval party.

'Many of those living near the coast had actually seen or heard of the accident, and were therefore already aware, without being warned, that there might be an opportunity of rendering assistance and possibly of saving life south of Marwick Head', is the assertion made in the White Paper.

This is totally inaccurate. The explosion could certainly not have been heard by anyone indoors in Birsay, and in such weather and at that hour most Orcadians were indoors. Hardly any of them were told of the incident either by neighbours or by the authorities. 'Had we been told that the *Hampshire* had sunk,' said one crofter, 'we could have provided signal lanterns and ropes for the men who struggled ashore. We could have waded in with lines and prevented the rafts from being hurled on the rocks. It wouldn't have been easy, but I reckon another fifty lives could have been saved.'

Why, if, as the Admiralty allege, the civilians were to be asked to help in the rescue, was not a message to this effect sent to the look-out post at Birsay? This is a sparsely populated part of the coast: only one half of the sixty-seven islands which form the Orkney group are inhabited. But there were enough people in the vicinity of Birsay to form a search party speedily, had they been alerted. The crofters, fowlers and fishermen who formed the population here had for centuries taken part in rescue operations. They had invaluable local knowledge of conditions, tides, currents and whirlpools.

Sir Walter Scott made the acquaintance of a very old woman who lived near Stromness, one Bessie Millar, who 'eked out an existence by selling favourable winds to mariners, for which her fee was sixpence'. And hardly a mariner sailed to sea from Stromness without visiting and paying his fee to Bessie Millar. She was the prototype of 'Norma of the Fitful Head' in Scott's book, *The Pirate*. Crofters, men and women alike, all possessed considerably more than a rudimentary knowledge of seamanship.

Mrs. Sabiston, of Skedge, Birsay, writes: 'We were living in the parish of Sandwick at the time the *Hampshire* went down. We did not see her sink and knew nothing about it until after midnight there came a loud knock at the door and someone shouted:

' "Are there any men here to help? Our ship has gone down".'

*   *   *   *   *

The man who had knocked at the door was Able Seaman John Robert Bowman, who is still alive at East Ruston, near Stalham in Norfolk.

Undoubtedly he owes his life to the prompt action and attention provided by Mrs. Sabiston's parents.

'We got out of bed at once—my parents and myself—and did what we could,' says Mrs. Sabiston. 'By the time we got a fire burning another sailor arrived. He was Dick Simpson and belonged to Tynemouth. It was sad that, after being rescued from the *Hampshire*, he was lost in action very shortly afterwards. His parents were both down here at the unveiling of the

Kitchener Memorial. They wrote to us up to the time of their death.'

Mrs. Sabiston does not minimise the severity of the storm. 'It was a night you would hardly expect to see at that time of year. The men certainly had little chance in such weather. It was no easy task for them to land rafts along such a high rugged shore.'

But, she adds, 'had the men around us known about the ship going down, they could have done quite a lot to save those who came ashore. Many died from exposure.'

Mrs. Sabiston will never forget the ordeal of June 5–6: 'I was up all night making tea and meals.'

In most cases it was the survivors themselves who first told the Orcadians what had happened. Farnden was one of them. He, too, reached the top of the cliffs, bruised and bleeding. He remembered little more than crawling towards a cottage and being given a hot drink and warm blankets by a family of crofters.

Wesson, when he came ashore could not even manage to speak until after he had been taken inside a cottage and put to bed with hot water bottles. His throat was constricted, his tongue parched and taut.

'Lie quite still,' he was told, 'and we'll get you a drink.'

It had not yet dawned on the crofter in this cottage that a ship had sunk near by. He had been indoors all night and knew nothing about the disaster. But he sent his daughter to fetch another crofter from a neighbouring cottage. By the time she came back Wesson was just able to let them know that a ship had sunk and other survivors might be on the rocks below.

The crofters lost no time. With lanterns and ropes they hurried to the rescue. Presently they came across Phillips. He was nearly unconscious. By the time they had taken him back to one of the cottages he was blue with cold and dangerously near to death.

'When I awoke, I was in bed, with another shipmate by my side. It was some time before I realised what had happened.

Then I heard the patter of wooden clogs and I tried to call out, but couldn't.

'Presently a woman opened the door and peeped in at us. I think she was astonished to find us alive.'

Meanwhile two more survivors had been found and put to bed in the adjoining room. All four were from the same raft.

Phillips claimed he was told by the crofter that he and other men had watched the progress of the three rafts drifting inshore until darkness came. Then, using their knowledge of the coast and currents, they stayed where they thought the rafts were most likely to strike the shore. At one o'clock in the morning they heard a crash against the rocks and found a raft. Then they hauled the survivors up the cliff.

This story does not, however, tally with that told by other survivors. Wesson insisted that he found his own way up the cliff, and, as has already been noted, was the first to tell the crofter what had happened. Rogerson, too, survived by his own efforts: 'seeing a house in the distance, I crawled to it and tried to wake the occupants. After shouting for about ten minutes I got an answer . . . I managed to make them understand about my shipmates, and rescue parties then went to the cliffs and saved all they could.'

Warrant Mechanician William Bennet, Bowman and Petty Officer Sweeney corroborated this.

The probability is that Phillips regained consciousness much later than he imagined, and by that time it was getting light and rescue operations were under way. A Naval surgeon told Phillips that had he 'been in the water another five minutes, death would have claimed him'.

Some of the survivors lost count of time while on the rafts. A few talked about being in the water ten hours and seeing dawn arrive. This was an illusion, due no doubt to the fact that in these northern waters in midsummer it is light until nearly 11 p.m.

Nevertheless, one farmer or crofter sighted three Carley floats—'boats', as he thought—drifting towards Skaill Bay. He lost sight of them when darkness came. He wanted to go down to Skaill Bay, or the rocks below Pallast, where he thought they would drift, but was ordered to return home by a Naval party in a car. Presumably this was the party which set off from Stromness. But, despite this information, the car moved off, not in the direction of Skaill Bay, but to Evie on the other side of the island.

Colonel Harris, Officer Commanding Troops, Kirkwall, was asked by the Admiral to go to Birsay to 'get first-hand information'. Why he was merely sent for this purpose when news could have been telegraphed from Birsay and when a Naval party had already set out is not clear. But then most actions were incomprehensible that night. Colonel Harris 'reached Birsay,' says the White Paper, 'after struggling for more than two hours against the gale.' From Birsay he proceeded to Skaill Bay, arriving there about 2.45 a.m. on June 6, 'by which time all but two of the survivors had been discovered'.

Captain Mackay, of the R.G.A. at Stromness, showed more initiative. As soon as he heard the news of the sinking he went to his superior officer, Colonel Brook, and told him what had happened.

'Can I go out and help?' asked Mackay.

'I am afraid I cannot give you an official order,' was the reply, 'but if you leave enough men behind to keep the battery in action, you can, if you wish, on your own responsibility, of course, go ahead. I leave the decision to you.'

Captain Mackay mustered his men, borrowed a car and took a small rescue party of Territorials out to Skaill Bay, dropping off two men on the way to search the coast northwards from Yescanaby. When they arrived there they learned that survivors had been washed ashore, had crawled up on to the Links and lawn in front of Skaill House and died of exposure, unnoticed.

The residents at Skaill House, Mrs. Watt, her daugher and servants and all their farm hands had slept soundly throughout the night without knowing what had happened.

5

Twelve Men Survived

OUT of the whole ship's company twelve men only survived.

It was a miracle that, with no aid from sea or land, anyone at all lived through the storm to scale the cliffs to safety.

When Jellicoe first flashed his signal about the *Hampshire*'s fate to the Admiralty, he was pessimistic: 'As the whole shore has been searched from the seaward, I greatly fear there is little hope of there being any survivors. No report has yet been received from the search party on shore.'*

Here is further evidence of the slowness of the rescue parties in getting off the mark. The Commander-in-Chief had a very incomplete picture of what had happened. Bit by bit the story of the tragedy was pieced together, but for many days it was a disconnected, puzzling story.

Jellicoe's first report stated that the cruiser was sunk 'either by a mine or a torpedo'. The fact was that some of his staff refused to accept the possibility of mines having been laid in that area. The preliminary report of the Commander-in-Chief also mentioned that 'four boats were seen by observers to leave the ship'. This, as the survivors testified, was wrong. No boats left the ship except the one which was smashed up as it was launched. The 'boats' were the rafts.

There is a footnote in the Admiralty White Paper which refers to this: 'Certain contemporary narratives by survivors

*This signal was received by the Admiralty at 10.30 a.m. (B.S.T.) on June 6.

(copies of which are in the possession of the Admiralty) were circulated to the Press from a private source in June, 1916, but not published. These narratives, it would seem, *wilfully garbled*, have been used as "survivors' stories" in some recent press articles on the loss of the *Hampshire*. Apparently the writer of these articles has not scrupled to insert from his own imagination whole sentences which were not in the original narratives.

'Another statement recently attributed to a survivor is that he saw Lord Kitchener in a boat. The Admiralty have satisfied themselves that the survivors did not see Lord Kitchener in a boat and never made any such statement.'

Ten days after the sinking an official Admiralty report included this: 'Efforts were made without success to lower some of the boats. . . . The Captain called out for Lord Kitchener to come up to the forebridge near where the Captain's boat was hoisted; he was also heard calling for Lord Kitchener to get into the boat, but no one is able to say whether Lord Kitchener got into the boat or not, nor what occurred to this boat; nor did anyone see any of the boats get clear of the ship.'

Whoever composed this statement was asking for trouble. It was just the sort of verbal fuel to feed the rumours which were beginning to circulate. Why, despite the testimony of such witnesses as Phillips, Farnden, Rogerson and Wesson, did the Admiralty suggest that there were any doubts as to whether Kitchener got into a boat or not?

The answer, although it was not admitted at the time, was that some survivors told a very different story. One survivor in particular was under the impression that he saw the captain's galley being lowered by hand. There was also a tendency at the Court of Inquiry to regard the evidence of the lower deck survivors as inaccurate.

An Admiralty statement, almost casually, referred to 'a private soldier' who 'appears to have left the ship on one of the rafts, but it is not known what became of him'.

This must have been the dying soldier whom Phillips saw. But the official reference to this man caused considerable confusion about the actual number of survivors. While the number of naval personnel totalled twelve, two Orcadian crofters insisted that a man in soldier's uniform was helped ashore. If so, he was not seen again. But this started the rumour that there were thirteen survivors and the mystery of the thirteenth was heightened by the fact that no one could identify him. Needless to say this raised hopes among uninformed civilians that it might be Kitchener.

All inquiries, however, confirm that while thirteen men were rescued, one died shortly afterwards. There is absolutely no confirmation about the mystery soldier. Several more died from exposure as they lay undiscovered, until at dawn the shore party came across their bodies.

Not a single officer survived. The fortunate twelve were:

WILLIAM BENNET, Warrant Mechanician.
JOHN ROBERT BOWMAN, A.B.
HORACE LLEWELLYN BUERDSELL, A.B.
WILLIAM CASHMAN, Leading Seaman.
WALTER CHARLES FARNDEN, Stoker.
WILLIAM CHARLES PHILLIPS, Shipwright.
ALFRED ERNEST READ, Stoker.
CHARLES WALTER ROGERSON, Leading Seaman.
RICHARD SIMPSON, A.B.
FREDERICK LOT SIMS, Stoker.
SAMUEL EDWARD SWEENEY, Petty Officer.
WILFRED WESSON, Petty Officer.

In the hours immediately before dawn the rescue ships searched in every direction along the coast. It has been stated that they used their searchlights not only over the sea, but on the coast, in the attempt to discover boats or rafts and in the hope of assisting the shore parties. If so, none of the civilians ashore saw these lights. On that point they are quite unanimous. One of the crew of the destroyer *Victor* said afterwards: 'We wanted to use searchlights, but were told it was too dangerous in wartime.'

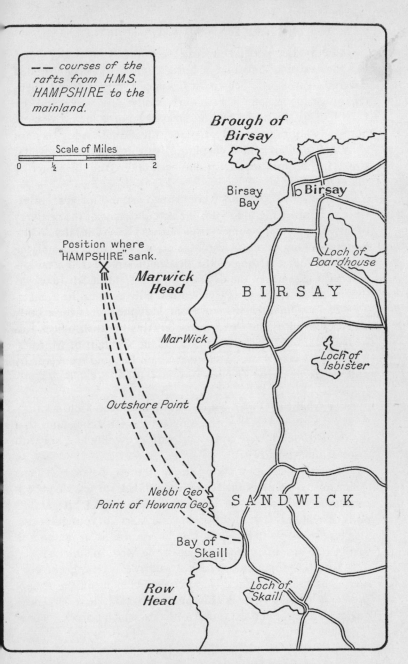

courses of the rafts from H.M.S. HAMPSHIRE to the mainland.

Scale of Miles
0   ½   1   2

Brough of Birsay

Birsay Bay

Birsay

Loch of Boardhouse

Position where "HAMPSHIRE" sank.

Marwick Head

B I R S A Y

MarWick

Loch of Isbister

Outshore Point

Nebbi Geo
Point of Howana Geo

S A N D W I C K

Bay of Skaill

Row Head

Loch of Skaill

Birsay and landing places of survivors

Many bodies were taken from the water by the rescue ships. But the bodies of only two of Lord Kitchener's party were discovered—those of Lieutenant-Colonel Fitzgerald and Lieutenant Macpherson. The latter's body was recovered by H.M.S. *Oak*, in which he had crossed from Thurso to Scapa not many hours previously. Colonel Fitzgerald's body was not identified until it had been placed with others in the hospital ship, H.M.S. *Soudan*, after it had been taken from the water by the *Flying Kestrel*.

As many wild rumours were bruited around for years afterwards about Fitzgerald's end, the actual details of the recovery of his body are of some importance. The Admiralty White Paper has this to say: 'The Master of this vessel (the *Flying Kestrel*) states that one of the first bodies recovered after she reached the scene of the disaster on the night of 5th June was that of an officer in khaki, which was conveyed to the *Soudan*. This cannot have been Lieutenant Macpherson, whose body was recovered by the *Oak*; moreover, this Scottish officer was wearing tartan trousers. Nor was it the Captain of Marines, whose body was washed ashore at Skaill Bay and recovered by a shore rescue party. The description, therefore, can only apply to Colonel Fitzgerald.

'The Medical Officer who actually identified Colonel Fitzgerald's body in the Hospital Ship on the 6th June states that the signs of death were consistent with drowning and not with death from exposure.

'The only reason for laying stress on these melancholy facts is because absolutely false and unfounded stories have been circulated with regard to the finding of Colonel Fitzgerald's body. The first is that the body showed marks of foul play—the alleged work of spies. This can be dismissed as without a vestige of truth, upon the evidence of the Medical Officer.

'The other story, which is equally untrue, is that this officer's body was found several days after the accident, in the *Hampshire*'s skiff dinghy, and this particular boat has, in consequence, been publicly exhibited as that in which Lord Kitchener and Colonel Fitzgerald left the *Hampshire*. There is no evidence that anyone entered the skiff dinghy after the accident, and it is known for certain that Colonel Fitzgerald's body was not found in it.'

The story that Fitzgerald was the victim of foul play was actually published in some newspapers both in Britain and abroad. It is quite unsubstantiated, though the following account by Skipper Davies of the *Flying Kestrel* may provide a clue to its origin:

'We picked up some thirty-two bodies about six miles south of where the *Hampshire* sank. Among them was that of Lieutenant-Colonel Fitzgerald.

'His body was spotted in the water and was brought aboard by lassooing it round the neck with a rope.

'Someone shouted out: "Is he dead?" and another replied: "If he hasn't been dead for hours, we've certainly hanged him now".'

Skipper Davies said there were lasso marks on the neck and that these may have started the rumour about foul play. But the Admiralty statement makes no reference to this evidence, which seems the most likely explanation of the rumours.

The rescue parties worked until late the following morning bringing up all the bodies from a float which had jammed in the rocks at Nebbi Geo. But it was not until 9 a.m. on June 6 that Colonel Harris, with a party of Territorials, returned from Kirkwall to Skaill Bay to collect the dead and bring them in on lorries for identification.

Mr. John Folsetter remembers seeing two lorry loads of bodies coming to Stromness Pier, little attempt being made to cover them from public view: some were almost naked. They were sent down a chute into the hold of a naval tug to be taken for burial at Lyness.

*   *   *   *   *

Lieutenant Boissier's party divided into two at Outshore Point, the main section searching the cliffs southwards, while the cars went on to Skaill Bay. The aim was for the two men in the cars to work northwards to rejoin the other section.

The White Paper says: 'The main party heard answering voices at Nebbi Geo, and found one survivor near the top of the cliff and three others at the bottom. With the assistance of some of the local inhabitants, these were hauled up and taken to a farmhouse.'

Yet William Phillips, one of the farmers and father of Mrs. Sabiston, tells a different story, which is confirmed by other crofters. Mr. Phillips, with other farmers, volunteered of his own accord to bring up as many men as he could. So a rope was tied round his waist and, while the other farmers held on to it, he secured the survivors one by one. 'We had rescued quite a few before the Naval party arrived.'

One raft had been hurled into a narrow V-shaped inlet. Owing to the severity of the storm it was impossible for the Naval party, so inadequately equipped and so few in numbers, to secure the raft. One man in it was still alive and was heard shouting to rescuers, but by the time they got him up the cliffs he had died.

It was not until the tide had receded that this raft was eventually secured and examined. By that time all those aboard were also dead.

Forty-two other men were found dead in a raft which had been lifted right over a high rock and had come to rest between ledges of rock some 300 yards south of the first raft at the northern entrance to Skaill Bay. 'We could have reached this, if we hadn't been turned away by the Naval party,' declared crofter McKay.

Captain Mackay's party of Territorials located the small float, which had overturned on the beach. The two survivors from this frail craft were found at daylight lying on the grass above the beach.

Searchlights ashore could have greatly facilitated the rescue work. Those who worked frantically in the darkness to free the float at Geo received a terrible buffeting from the waves and two of them collapsed.

Had the rafts drifted in a few hundred yards farther south, in Skaill Bay itself, perhaps sixty more lives could have been saved.

*   *   *   *   *

Shipwright Phillips could hardly believe he had escaped from the nightmare of the storm when he opened his eyes and found himself in the crofter's cottage. Still weak and faint with exhaustion, he staggered to his feet and stumbled around the room.

An object which seemed vaguely familiar lay on a table. Picking it up, Phillips recognised his leather purse. Inside it were his identity disc, a shilling piece and a Treasury note.

Later the crofter's wife told him that the note had been just a piece of sodden pulp. She had dried it carefully in front of the fire, then ironed it out and folded it up again before replacing it in the purse.

Phillips determined that the purse and its contents should be kept as a souvenir of his narrow escape from death. 'I was too thankful to have been saved, and perhaps too super-stitious as well, to change the money, or spend it.'

Later, with the aid of a stick, he walked round the neigh-bouring cottages to see the other survivors. Six had been rescued from one raft, four from the second and two from the small float. But the sight of the dead, laid out on top of the cliffs for identification, was too much for Phillips and he col-lapsed. Many bodies were horribly mangled as a result of being torn to pieces on the rocks.

Mr. John Sabiston helped two survivors who were taken in by a family at Gerricot. One of these was Samuel Sweeney. In the hearing of this family Sweeney asked: 'Why was that door open at that time?'

There was no elaboration of this cryptic remark, nor was there a reply, for Sweeney's companion held up his hand as though to silence further questions.

Sweeney himself is no longer alive to explain what he meant. Years later he committed suicide after having cut the throats of his wife and mother-in-law. Perhaps the events of that night affected his mind.

But crofter McKay testified that another survivor moaned in his delirium: 'Shut that bloody door! Why doesn't someone shut that bloody door? Who is it trying to kill us?'

The survivors were most hospitably cared for by the cottagers and some of them made friends for life of the kindly Orcadians. It was not until June 7 that the twelve men were taken to H.M.S. *Blake* in Scapa Flow, where later in the afternoon of that day the Court of Inquiry into the loss of the *Hampshire* was opened.

Phillips had a macabre experience when he came across an old shipmate in H.M.S. *Blake*. The latter rating was making coffins for the *Hampshire* victims, and, knowing that Phillips had served in the cruiser, he had somewhat ghoulishly anticipated the worst by carving Phillips' name on one of them.

*   *   *   *   *

'I have often wondered since that fatal day whether anything could have been done that was not done,' wrote Jellicoe. 'But short of postponing the departure of the *Hampshire* altogether, until weather conditions admitted of a channel being swept ahead of her, *no safeguards were possible*. Such a decision would have resulted in two or three days' delay in starting, and would never have been agreed to by Lord Kitchener.'

It was always said during 1916 that Jellicoe was the one man in Britain who could win or lose the war in a single afternoon. Never since has the fate of the nation been so much in the hands of one individual, who could, by a stroke of the pen, commit the whole of the Grand Fleet to perdition.

Jellicoe, in seeking to justify his handling of the sailing arrangements for the *Hampshire*, commented: 'I should not have hesitated, if need had arisen, to take the Grand Fleet to sea on the same night and by the same route as that traversed by the *Hampshire*.'*

*The Grand Fleet.

This is an astonishing statement, possibly the most-Bala-clava-minded piece of nonsense which ever came from the lips of a British admiral. In effect it means that Jellicoe would have sailed the Grand Fleet on an unswept route in mine-infested waters, hugging the coast and making his big ships a sitting target for enemy submarines. In a gale like this, he could not have relied on speed to beat the submarines. Even the *Hampshire*, which started off at full speed, was forced to reduce to $13\frac{1}{2}$ knots at the time of the disaster.

6

'So Much Loose Talk'

WHEN Fleet Street received the Press Association announcement that Kitchener had gone down with the *Hampshire*, Hannen Swaffer telephoned his chief, Lord Northcliffe, to pass on the news.

The comment of that ruthless press lord was laconic and typical: 'Well, Swaffer, now we can at last get down to winning the war.'

But Northcliffe's sentiments were not those of the vast majority of his fellow-countrymen. Throughout the holocaust of incessant slaughter in World War I no other single death so profoundly shocked the British people as a whole, or lowered morale so much, as the loss of that proud and authoritarian figure whose face stared down at them from ten thousand poster hoardings.

The grim tidings were repeated in hushed whispers in the streets; in cafés, clubs and public houses, across the tea tables and in the canteens the news silenced chatter and laughter.

'People snatched at the newspapers and tore the sheets in their anger,' said the *Daily Dispatch*. 'The announcement had a stunning effect. In the West End the blinds were drawn.'

Nor was this journalistic hyperbole; newspapers were more sober in those days. Some businesses and shops put up their shutters for the day. In many towns curtains were drawn across all the windows of suburban houses and pathetic little Union

Jacks were hoisted in tiny front gardens, only to be lowered to half-mast.

It might have been the Sovereign who had died. And, indeed, the King himself was as grieved as his subjects, for Kitchener was his personal friend. And on George V's orders officers of the Army were instructed to wear mourning bands for a whole week.

A coroner, summing up at an inquest in Yorkshire, recorded that 'the deceased seems to have become very depressed after learning of the death of Lord Kitchener, and subsequently to have taken his life.'

Not even when the truth about the casualties on the Somme filtered through the censorship were people everywhere so bewildered and downcast as in this June of 1916. Kitchener's passing marked the end of an era.

All this may seem strangely out of keeping with the normal phlegm of the British people. More strange still when one knows that not so long before Kitchener died, Lloyd George (then Minister of Munitions) told Max Aitken (now Lord Beaverbrook): 'Kitchener talked absolute twaddle, Max. No, that's not quite right. Let me put it this way: he has a mind like a revolving lighthouse. Sometimes the beam lights up all Europe and the opposing armies in vast and illimitable perspective. Then the shutter comes round and for several weeks you get blank darkness.'

Although in the last few months of his life Kitchener's reputation among the politicians had been somewhat tarnished, to the public he remained a hero to the last. Typical of this hero-worship is a story, told by Sir George Arthur. He recalled how a young private was found dead in the Flanders trenches, one hand clasping a rifle and the other a torn, blood-stained photograph of Kitchener. Such was the pathetic faith which was conjured up by this monolithic man who presided over the War Office.

With his passing Britain lost the last of her great pro-Consuls and perhaps the last and most remarkable Empire-builder of modern times. In his lifetime Kitchener had become the Father-Image of the nation, a legend of a supreme and invincible warrior. Yet he had no nickname to project him to the masses, like 'Bobs' Roberts, and he was the very reverse of the normal type of popular hero—morose, uncommunicative, suspicious and unbending, a man who rarely smiled. Nevertheless, that face on the hoardings with its exhortation—'Your country needs YOU'—while portraying the tough, Orwellesque' Big Brother' of the patriotic school, had swayed hundreds of thousands to join the Colours in a psychological propaganda drive that not even television could achieve today.

'The Constable of Britain', Winston Churchill had called him. And indeed from the moment that the Prime Minister, Asquith, summoned him to No. 10 Downing Street, on August 3, 1914, from the cross-channel ship at Dover, in which he was about to make the first stage of his journey back to Egypt, Kitchener was for a whole year the most powerful man in the country.

Asquith, who could make decisions as swiftly as any man when he wished, decided that a non-party, popular military figure was best fitted to the office of Secretary of State for War, that traditional graveyard of so many civilian politicians' hopes. With the threat of civil war in Ulster still smouldering in the background, with generals in their clubs plotting against the Liberal Government, this was undoubtedly a stroke of genius on Asquith's part. Kitchener's appointment silenced all the critics and, of greater importance, quelled the talkative and hysterical pro-Ulster generals.

Between the two world wars Kitchener was as often derided as in 1914 he was hailed and lauded. He has been depicted as the personification of rigid and unimaginative militarism and accused of being particularly inept in the political field. He had his defects; he was saturnine, shy, silent and secretive. He had been away from Britain too long to be easily acclimatised to political processes. Personality and authority he had to a high degree, but he lacked charm and made no effort to acquire friends.

Yet in perspective he appears to have been a much greater man and a far abler soldier than his critics would have us believe. Perhaps the public sensed this greatness more accurately than some politicians. He possessed the valuable asset for a soldier-turned-statesman of being immune from the temptations to intrigue. To the few friends he had he was loyal to a fault. At no time during World War II did any other military leader emerge who commanded the same respect and trust among the people. Whatever his faults, he could justly claim that in 1914 he was nearly always right, when every other general and most politicians were very far out in their assessments of military prospects.

Horatio Herbert Kitchener started his career as War Minister with almost Churchillian far-sightedness. If he erred in underestimating the organisation of the Territorial Army carried out by Lord Haldane, he was equally mistrustful of the advice tendered to him by his soldier colleagues. When his aides at the War Office insisted that no modern war could possibly last a year and that 50,000 soldiers were enough for a volunteer army, he gave them a scathing look, said nothing, but added a nought on to their draft for a recruiting appeal.

Within the first week of coming to office he forecast that it would be a long war and overruled those—Lloyd George was among them—who said it would be finished in nine months. 'The Chancellor of the Exchequer will find that war is not a matter of simple gestation,' he told the Cabinet. 'It will last for three to four years.'

But the people knew nothing of these matters, any more than they knew of the despicable sniping at the War Minister behind his back by Bonar Law, Edward Carson and Lloyd George. The people's picture of Kitchener was a more romantic one, etched in the decade before when, in Africa and India, he strode like a Titan across the imperial arena. Perhaps they instinctively associated him with that other lonely figure of Victorian

L.K.D.—F

days, who died as a result of ministerial incompetence—General Gordon. For there were certain resemblances between Kitchener and Gordon—their dislike of women, their passion for religion, their campaigns in Africa, their eccentricities and aloofness. In 1914–16 there was still a deep-rooted, passionate belief in the British Empire among the masses, and a mystical faith in its exponents.

Such a faith was based on commonsense as well as romanticism. Had not the Empire brought prosperity which, if not shared among the masses, could at least be seen by them and made them feel superior to the proletariat on the Continent? And Kitchener had proved himself not merely an expert on logistics and the victor of Omdurman, but as a statesman who had made a study of Ottoman law, who had in two years' fighting in his Sudanese campaign added a million or more square miles to the Colonial Empire for a cost of only £2,413,213—'what I call economic soldiering' had been his own comment on this achievement.

For years after June 5, 1916, people recalled that such and such a thing happened 'the day Kitchener was drowned'. For many people in their early middle age today it is one of their earliest recollections. But when a man becomes a legend in his life-time there is a tendency to regard him as immortal. Weaker-minded romantics refused to accept his death as a fact. Nineteen years later there was a vociferous minority who insisted that T. E. Lawrence was not killed in a motor-cycling accident, but that he had merely 'disappeared' to go on a secret mission to Abyssinia.

Kitchener was similarly, in legend, preserved from death. His hold on the public imagination was so strong that many refused to accept the official announcement of his passing. So imagination gave birth to rumour and soon it was whispered that he had been picked up by a submarine and taken prisoner, or that he was living as a hermit on a lonely island, that he was in Russia directing a new offensive against the Germans, and that his death had been announced by the Cabinet to fool the

Kaiser. He was variously reported as appearing in Cairo, Cyprus, Rome and Washington.

It was odd, people argued, that, if Kitchener were dead, his body had not been recovered. Kitchener had had a charmed life, he had escaped assassination on countless occasions. When he was wounded in the throat in a clash with Digna's Dervishes, he amazed even his surgeon by swallowing the bullet and passing it out by normal physical processes the next day. Besides, they explained to their listeners, Kitchener was a strong swimmer; had he not saved a brother officer from drowning at Ascalon under very difficult conditions? Had he not in the past undertaken intelligence work and was he not just the type who would disappear for a while to bring off some Secret Service coup?

But the Brough of Birsay was not Ascalon and Kitchener so hated the cold climate of Britain after years in the East that he would not have bathed in the sea off these coasts even in summer time. When the first wave of optimism receded and it was realised that Kitchener had in fact been drowned, an angry reaction set in. It was disgraceful, said the Kitchener-worshippers; it was nothing short of treachery that a man so vital to the war effort should be allowed to go to his death by the Government. There must be some blunder somewhere. How did it happen? And, once that question was asked, and left unanswered by war-time officialdom, the rumour-mongers, aided by the lunatic fringe of the population, supplied the answers and named the culprits.

The answers were as varied and Munchausen-like as the stories that Kitchener was still alive. Up and down the country people were attributing his death to a plot engineered by one or more of the following—the Prime Minister, Mrs. Asquith, Admiral Jellicoe, Lord Haldane, Lord Northcliffe, Trebitsch Lincoln, Colonel Repington (Military Correspondent of *The Times*), and Lloyd George.

The wildness of these rumours illustrates the mixture of war hysteria and wavering morale which typified certain periods of the 1914–18 war. The latter half of 1916 was such a period. Kitchener's death contributed in several ways, direct and indirect, to the gradual disintegration of the Asquith administration. Tories and Lloyd Georgian Liberals attributed the *Hampshire* episode to the incompetence of the Government: it was a useful, though contemptible piece of political propaganda at a time when the Government was suffering from a series of setbacks. The urge to make party capital out of the misfortunes of the Government was much greater in World War I than in World War II, and by their use of the *Hampshire* disaster to gain political advantage, many Tories earned merited contempt.

Mrs. Asquith, a frank-speaking woman, who maintained throughout the war that one did not have to hate all Germans just because one was at war with them, paid for her high-mindedness by being perpetually singled out as a pro-German. She recorded in her diary that 'The D——ss of W—— and others continue spreading amazing lies about me and mine. Elizabeth (her daughter) is in turn engaged to a German admiral or a German general; Henry (her husband) has shares in Krupps; I feed Prussian prisoners with every dainty comestible and play lawn tennis with them at Donnington Hall—a place whose very whereabouts is unknown to me.'

Lord Haldane was dubbed as pro-German because of his education at Heidelberg and as a direct result of his once having said that 'Germany is my spiritual home', a reference to his keen interest in Teutonic philosophy. In his autobiography Lord Haldane told how 'my motives and the nature of my efforts when I went to Berlin in 1912 were grossly misrepresented in some newspapers. Every kind of ridiculous legend about me was circulated. I had a German wife; I was the illegitimate brother of the Kaiser; I had been in secret correspondence with the German government . . . on one day, in response to an appeal in the *Daily Express*, there arrived at the House of Lords no less than 2,000 letters of protest against my supposed disloyalty to the interest of the nation . . . I had gone to Germany too often, and had read her literature too much, not to give ground to narrow-minded people to say that Germany was my "spiritual home".'

As for Lord Northcliffe, apart from the comment to Hannen Swaffer already mentioned, he was a notorious Kitchener-hater. Once he inveighed in a frenzied rage about the War Minister: 'Sack him! He's murdered my nephew!' Northcliffe could never understand why politicians did not sack generals with the same ruthlessness and paranoiac frenzy that he showed in peremptorily dismissing his own terrorised reporters.

Colonel Repington was an ally of Northcliffe, and regarded by some as a dangerous intriguer who was out for Kitchener's scalp; but although Northcliffe in certain moods would have unhesitatingly ordered Kitchener to be shot (had any politician been rash enough to give him such powers), Repington was on the whole a fair-minded, honest critic who eventually risked his career in the cause of fearless journalism. When he left *The Times* and joined the *Morning Post*, he revealed the secret plan to put the General Reserve under Foch's orders. It was an open challenge to the Lloyd George administration, and Repington was charged and fined for a breach of the Defence Regulations.

By a coincidence on the very day that Kitchener travelled north to join the *Hampshire* there arrived at Liverpool aboard the *Cameronia* Trebitsch Lincoln, the former Member of Parliament for Darlington, who had become a German spy. Previously Lincoln fled to the United States when the Admiralty and M.I.5 began to examine reports that he was acting as an agent for the Germans. There he blatantly contacted the German Consulate and defiantly published *The Revelations of an International Spy*. Then the British Government secured his extradition from U.S.A. and he was brought back to Britain to face a charge of fraud.

It required little imagination on the part of sensation hunters to suggest there was some sinister link between Kitchener's death and Lincoln's arrival back in Britain, despite the fact that the latter was under close arrest.

Admiral Jellicoe suffered keenly the barbs of bitter tongues and much malicious talk. In a final assessment of who was responsible for the loss of the *Hampshire*, he must inevitably take some of the blame. A man of honour and integrity, he never was a brilliant naval leader. But he did not deserve the cruel innuendoes levelled against him.

Of more interest were the accusations made against Lloyd George, which, though seemingly more fantastic than any, deserve examination, and will be dealt with in another chapter.

Superficially, it might seem there is little point in resurrecting these nearly forgotten, fatuous scraps of scandal. The truth is that it was the lunatic lengths to which the scandal purveyors went which finally forced the story of Kitchener and the *Hampshire* into oblivion. But sometimes facts—particularly unpalatable facts—can be conveniently buried beneath the sands of fantasy. Once one has sifted these sands, and rebutted the absurdities and extravaganzas, there emerges a picture, however incomplete, of fact as remarkable and even as grotesque as any of the fantasies which were woven around the Kitchener legend.

A preliminary study of the episode of the sinking of the *Hampshire* quickly reveals a tangle of contradictions and half-truths. Consecutive British governments in the past forty years have contributed to the air of mystery by their reticence, and in some instances downright refusal, to make facts public. It was the obvious course to adopt while war was being waged; it was even understandable, though not necessarily justifiable, in the years immediately after that war. But today such a policy is incomprehensible.

When I set out to write this book, I did not imagine that there could be any reason why the Admiralty should not allow me access to their documents on the loss of the *Hampshire*. My early researches suggested that Admiralty White Paper Cmd. 2710 by no means gave all the facts available and was, in some instances, unsatisfactory and evasive. It also seemed only right that, if by producing further evidence and documents the

Admiralty could satisfactorily answer the many unsolved mysteries of the *Hampshire* episode, they should in the interests of truth have the opportunity of doing so.

I therefore made a formal approach to the Admiralty. The reply was that I could be granted facilities for the inspection of official records in connection with the preparation of a book about the death of Lord Kitchener in H.M.S. *Hampshire* on condition that I forwarded the draft to the Admiralty for scrutiny and amended the text 'as may be required for reasons of public interest' before publication.

I replied that I was quite prepared to submit the draft of my book and would undertake to delete any material from Admiralty sources which it was considered undesirable to reproduce. I added that I would even be prepared to delete any material which I had obtained independently of the Admiralty, if such material was included in their records and they did not wish it to be made public. But on one point I was adamant. If I obtained material from independent sources which was not to be found in Admiralty records, I maintained that I ought to be at liberty to publish it. With this one proviso, I was prepared to accede to the Admiralty conditions.

It was as well I made this proviso, for the Admiralty's further reply was to the effect that I would be required to submit the whole of my manuscript and to amend any part of it for 'reasons of public interest, regardless of the source from which your information is obtained.'

The risks of acceding to such conditions were obvious—the book could be rejected in its entirety by the Admiralty; it could be so mutilated as to be no better than an emasculated version of the original.

I felt that I could no more accept these conditions today than could Sir George Arthur thirty-five years ago.

For that reason the only Admiralty viewpoint that can be presented in this book is that contained in the White Paper. Despite allegations of treachery, governmental ineptitude and criminal negligence made in the country and in Parliament for years after the war, it was not until August, 1926, that the Admiralty issued in the White Paper, the official narrative of the events which led up to the death of the War Minister. Parliament was not, of course, then sitting. By the time members returned to Westminster the White Paper had been almost forgotten and no more questions were asked.

Before its publication, the *Daily Express* stated in its leader column of April 7, 1926: 'Despite statements by Ministers and answers in the House of Commons there is still a large number of people who suspect that the loss of the *Hampshire* in 1916 was due to Naval treachery. The widespread nature of this suspicion is shown in public meetings and newspaper correspondence. Perhaps it has been fostered most of all by the Admiralty's refusal to publish the report of the Naval Court of Inquiry, on the grounds that such reports must always be inviolable.'

How was it that ten years after Kitchener's death these suspicions and doubts prevailed? What caused the spate of rumours, letters to the press and questions asked in Parliament?

The first published hint of such doubts was the statement in *The Times* (then under Northcliffe's personal control) of June 7, 1916, that 'the possibility that news of Lord Kitchener's movements had been conveyed to the enemy by spies was widely discussed yesterday, and it is of interest that the official intimation in the *London Gazette* issued last night placed new restrictions on passengers landing at ports in the Orkneys.'

Three days later *The Times* mentioned that a wireless message from Berne alleged that Lord Kitchener's intention of visiting Russia was known in Germany.

The rumours might yet have been silenced, had the Admiralty not persisted for so long in refusing to publish a report. What really aroused public interest after the war was the claim from Berlin that a German woman spy had been directly responsible for Kitchener's death. Branches of the British

Legion all over Britain raised the question in resolutions and pressed for a Government statement.

The Admiralty was consistently evasive. Even in February 1926, the First Lord, Mr. W. C. Bridgeman, in replying to questions from Sir Robert Hamilton, a Liberal M.P., and Mr. Patrick Hannon* (a Conservative), stated that 'there are valid objections to the publication of the report of Naval Courts of Inquiry into the loss of the *Hampshire*.'

Yet there was more than idle curiosity on the part of the public and some members of Parliament. Allied governments had been concerned about rumours of treachery and both the French and United States intelligence services had intimation from reliable agents that the news of Kitchener's departure had been passed to the Germans, and that treachery was suspected.

It was at this stage that Lord Kitchener's friend and biographer intervened. In his *Life of Lord Kitchener*, Sir George Arthur wrote this about his hero's end: 'By an unhappy error of judgement an unswept channel was chosen for the passage of the cruiser and Kitchener—*the secret of whose journey had been betrayed*—was to fall into the machinations of England's enemies and to die swiftly at their hands.'

Then, in the midst of all the post-war controversy about the sinking of the cruiser, Sir George Arthur wrote to *The Times* on February 10, 1926:

'There is so much loose talk and so many questions are addressed to me with regard to the death of Lord Kitchener that I would ask you to let me say that early in 1920 the First Lord of the Admiralty (the late Lord Long) asked me to read the secret or unpublished report on the sinking of the *Hampshire* on the understanding that I would not divulge a word to anybody.

'I declined to read the document under these conditions, as my object was to give in my *Life of Lord Kitchener* the correct version of the tragedy, and this I could not do if the material were in my hands which I was not allowed to use. I told the

*Later Sir Patrick Hannon.

First Lord that I should submit that neglect, or at any rate carelessness must be charged to the Admiralty, or the Commander of the Grand Fleet in the arrangements made for Lord Kitchener's voyage. The reply of the First Lord was: "I do not think you could say otherwise".'

So, on the evidence of Sir George Arthur, a meticulous, if not an objective biographer, substantiated by a First Lord of the Admiralty, it appears that carelessness was at least in some degree a cause of Kitchener's death.

The negative attitude adopted by each British Government over a period of ten years not unnaturally fanned the flames of rumour. Soon it was not only suggested that treachery and negligence had caused the sinking of the cruiser; doubts were even cast on the official statement that she had struck a mine. Reports from Austria and Germany claimed that bombs had been placed aboard the ship and that her destruction was the work of saboteurs. To complicate matters two individuals claimed to have been personally responsible for placing the bombs and sinking the ship. Nor did they make these claims anonymously; they wrote lengthy and detailed accounts of their actions and signed them in their true names.

The story of the *Hampshire*'s end has now been told. But there remains the enigma of the Admiralty's reticence on the subject. Therefore it is necessary to sift fact from fiction and to re-examine the available evidence. For it is an inescapable fact that three vital questions have never been satisfactorily answered, either by the Admiralty White Paper, or by Kitchener's biographers.

These questions are:

(1) Was there criminal carelessness and treachery which led to the sinking of the *Hampshire*?

(2) Was there a secret and unpublished report on the whole affair which could tell a very different story from any heard yet?

(3) How exactly did the cruiser meet her doom?

7

Mission to Russia

VIOLENT political upheavals in Russia were in the first place responsible for the proposed Kitchener mission to Petrograd in the midsummer of 1916.

In August, 1914, Russian feats of arms in the east had eased the relentless pressure of the German war machine on the western front and so saved Britain and France from disaster. Yet early in 1916 it had become apparent that the situation was reversed: Russian ineptitude, corruption and defeatism threatened to lose the war for the Allies.

Materially it was a question of a grave shortage of munitions in the hard-pushed Russian armies, but spiritually it went much deeper than that. The drug of nihilism had somnambulised the people, forming a vast vacuum of numbed humanity between the Czarist régime and the old traditions of revolutionary liberalism. In that vacuum of despair and fatalistic acceptance of suffering, communism, through its Teutonic agents, began to operate like some giant bee-hive. But the real tragedy of Russia was the failure of the Government to realise that the true patriots, the men who could have supplied the energy and drive necessary to combat corruption and achieve victory were the despised revolutionaries. Not the communist agents who carried on their work almost unhindered, but men like Savinkov and Miliukov, who, despite their fanatical advocacy of terrorist methods, were vehement and sincere opponents of German militarism.

When Czarism was overthrown and mortal crisis confronted the broken ranks of Imperial Russia, these diametrically opposed forces came together and the Czar's Foreign Minister, M. de Sazonov, was able to say of Savinkov, the bomb thrower: 'I am astonished to be working with him, but he is a man most competent, full of resource and resolution. No one is so good.'

Savinkov was in the nihilist tradition. His whole life had been used as a revolutionary, plotting against the Czar, using sabotage and violence. Yet in his greatest hour he became the spearhead of the loyalists, working faithfully and unflinchingly with the very men he had previously sought to destroy. But by then it was too late.

In Britain from the Foreign Office right down to the man-in-the-street there was an almost callous lack of interest in Russia. She was regarded with indifference and suspicion. Sir Edward Grey had always taken the realistic view that as an ally Russia was essential for British survival in any continental war. But his staff at the Foreign Office did little to preserve and implement the fundamentals of the Triple Alliance of Britain, France and Russia as far as the last-named was concerned.

Kitchener, more than most of his colleagues, had always taken the keenest interest in Russian affairs and in consequence had long foreseen the possibility of the collapse of her armies. Convinced that the fate of Russia was of overriding importance to the Allies, he had warned the Cabinet of the dangers of underground forces trying to compel the Russians to make a deal with Germany and seek a separate armistice.

This viewpoint was consistently opposed by Lloyd George, then Minister of Munitions, whose opinions on Russia were prejudiced by his detestation of the Czarist régime. He had always been a bitter opponent of Sir Edward Grey's efforts to establish an *entente* with the Court of the Czar. Whereas Churchill, an implacable enemy of Communism, set aside his prejudices in World War II and strove to establish mutual trust with the Soviet Government, not even the fact that Britain and Russia were allies altered Lloyd George's outlook on the Czarists. Kitchener stressed the need to give Russia greater military support and criticised the failure of Lloyd George to keep his promises of greater arms supplies for the Imperial armies, just as in World War II Churchill nagged and goaded the Chiefs of Staff until they reluctantly agreed to send the tanks which ultimately helped to save Stalingrad from the enemy. But Lloyd George insisted that, if supplies of munitions in excess of what could be legitimately spared were poured into Russia, they might be used against Britain on some future occasion.

Speaking before the Royal Commission on the Private Manufacture of Armaments in 1936, Lloyd George declared: 'Undertakings were given by our armament firms to the Russians with even worse results. Not even any appreciable percentage of the obligations undertaken was ever discharged. The Russians depended upon them and found themselves with no means of defending their lives against the German attack. The feeling against the British firms was, as I know, exceedingly bitter in the Russian army. The failure was attributed to the Russian collapse and disgruntlement with the Allies.'

In making this statement in 1936, Lloyd George, while putting the blame on 'the British firms', was, without frankly admitting it, providing proof of his own culpability in this matter. For the responsibility for supplying the Russians was clearly his. And he was the chief opponent in the Cabinet of sending further supplies to Russia.

Kitchener's reputation in military circles in Petrograd was high and his influence and opinions carried much weight with the Czar. Through diplomatic channels the Czar indicated that he would welcome a visit from the British War Minister. Early in May 1916, he sent a secret invitation to Kitchener, while at the same time a confidential approach was made to the British Government to obtain their approval of the project. It is certain that the initiative for this had come in the first place from

Kitchener, and that he had been making overtures to the Czar or someone close to that monarch. For the Russian Ambassador in Holland told the British Ambassador in Amsterdam that : 'Lord Kitchener's urgent representations and inspiriting messages have induced the Czar to consider the whole matter of *munitions supplies* from a new angle. The Czar now believes that a visit from Lord Kitchener can boost morale in Russia among the fainthearts at the Court. The Czar wants advice and he thinks it might help if the control of *certain things, possibly supplies*, were taken into British hands.'

Note the emphasis on munitions and supplies generally. This would normally be a question for the Minister of Munitions. But Lloyd George, no friend of the Russian Government, would obviously be an impediment to any plan to gratify the wishes of the Czar. It rather looks as though Kitchener had decided to take independent action, and, by communicating unofficially with the Czar, possibly to force Lloyd George's hand.

There are various and contradictory versions of this proposal to send a mission to Moscow. The Prime Minister, mindful of Kitchener's personal influence with the Czar and his high standing with Russian generals, strongly urged the acceptance of the invitation from Petrograd to the War Minister.

On the other hand Dr. Thomas Jones stated in his book *Lloyd George* that in April 1916, 'Asquith thought that Lloyd George should go to Russia. For some days the composition of the mission was in doubt, until Asquith decided the matter by announcing in the House of Commons on May 25 that the Minister of Munitions had agreed to devote his energies to the promotion of an Irish settlement, which had been newly bedevilled by the Easter Rebellion.'

This can hardly be correct, as in April the question of a visit to Russia had not formally been raised. Presumably Dr. Jones was basing his assumption on the fact that two days after the Commons announcement about Lloyd George's Irish negotiations a secret reply was dispatched to the Chief of the Military Mission in Russia stating that Kitchener hoped to arrive in Archangel on June 9. But, bearing in mind that Dr. Jones was working directly under Lloyd George at this period and that he was not addicted to making unsubstantiated statements, one must also assume that Lloyd George told him that he intended going to Russia.

Asquith was Kitchener's most loyal supporter in the Cabinet, and, while fully alive to the War Minister's limitations, he had a high regard for his diplomacy. If anyone could influence the Russians and persuade them to sink political differences and form a genuinely national government, then he felt that Kitchener, as a soldier, could do this better than any politician. Asquith's faith in Kitchener's ability was to some extent confirmed later by Miliukov (a revolutionary leader), who expressed the opinion that if Kitchener had been able to talk to the Russian Opposition leaders 'his renown as a soldier might have persuaded them to delay the revolution until after the war. But a mere politician could not have done this.'

Mr. Malcolm Thomson's version is that 'Lloyd George was planning to visit Russia with Kitchener. The Easter Rebellion upset this plan and Kitchener had to go alone at the last moment.' Mr. W. F. Burbidge in *Wizard of Wales* wrote: 'Lloyd George was invited to accompany this mission (to Russia), but because of his interest in the problems of the Irish question he declined.'

Lloyd George in his *War Memoirs* said that, but for a letter from Asquith, he would have gone with Kitchener in the *Hampshire* and lost his life. He was 'asked to take up Ireland, at any rate for a short time'.

And, summing up, Lloyd George added: 'That letter saved my life. Much against my own inclination I decided I could not refuse Mr. Asquith's request, so I had to tell Lord Kitchener I could not accompany him on his voyage.'

Lord Kitchener is not alive to confirm or deny this. Sir George Arthur had no knowledge that Lloyd George had been asked to go to Russia and considered it 'highly unlikely'. Lloyd George's Celtic propensity for convincing himself that the opposite to the truth is in fact the truth is well known. He hated the sea, was a bad sailor and a physical coward; it is unlikely that he would willingly have embarked on such a voyage. In none of Asquith's papers is there a reference to Lloyd George having been invited to go to Russia, either with or without Kitchener. It is highly unlikely that Kitchener would have acquiesced in having Lloyd George in the mission: the two men were constantly at loggerheads. And certainly Grey would have opposed the suggestion that Lloyd George should make the trip: the prospect of the Minister of Munitions, with his infinite capacity for interfering in foreign policy, visiting the Court of the Czar is not likely to have commended itself either to Asquith or Grey.

Only a few months earlier Lloyd George had dined with Colonel House, President Wilson's roving ambassador, and indiscreetly told him: 'The war can only be ended by the neutral intervention of President Wilson. This should come round about September next, when the slaughter that is now being planned rebounds on the heads of the planners and proves once again to be utterly ineffective. Terms should then be dictated by the President, terms which the belligerents would never agree upon if left to themselves.'

Fortunately, before he got in touch with the President, Colonel House repeated what Lloyd George had said to Balfour and Grey. They hastened to explain that this was quite contrary to British policy. This incident alone shows how dangerous it would have been to send Lloyd George to Russia.

Lloyd George's visit to Ireland had ended, and he was back in London, before Kitchener set off for Russia, so the alibi that it was the Irish Mission which caused his trip to Russia to be cancelled at the last moment does not hold. All the evidence seems to suggest that Lloyd George wished to give the impression that he intended going to Russia, though in fact he did not wish to go, and there was never any question of his going.

Even to his personal staff he gave this impression. At a few hours' notice he sent for Mr. Leslie Robertson, of the Ministry of Munitions, and deputed him to make the voyage with Kitchener. 'I find at the last moment I cannot go myself,' he added, 'so you will take my place.' Yet, according to his own statement in the *War Memoirs*, he had known he would not be going at least two weeks before this.

Two days after the sinking of the *Hampshire* it was stated in various British newspapers that 'Mr. Lloyd George nearly went with Lord Kitchener to Russia.' The source for this statement was Mr. Lloyd George himself, though he was not directly quoted.

Security arrangements for the mission to Russia were shared by the Foreign Office, the War Office and the Admiralty; officially it was treated as top secret. But in effect all attempts at security had broken down at least a month before the *Hampshire* sailed. For example, on May 6, 1916, Brigadier-General Ellershaw was writing to Major-General Knox (representing British interests in Petrograd) that 'I have very little doubt that shortly after you get this Lord Kitchener and I will be on our way to you.'

That letter was not sent in cipher.

There is, in fact, abundant evidence that many people in Britain, Russia, Germany and elsewhere knew of the intended mission some few weeks before it was to have been made. Early in May 1916 it was a common topic of conversation in the British Boat Club in Petrograd that Kitchener was leaving Britain early in June and was expected at Archangel on or about June 19. Sir George Arthur said that nearly a week before the Field-Marshal left London for Scapa Flow, 'I received a telegram from a non-official in Russia, asking if I was coming also.'

In Russian Court circles the subject of Kitchener's visit had been freely discussed and afterwards it was said that the German fiancée of a Russian officer, who was related to the House of Schleswig-Holstein, passed on the information to the German espionage organisation in Petrograd.

After the war an American, Mr. Ivar Hargreaves, who had been in Russia in the early summer of 1916, declared: 'It was nothing short of scandalous that so many people not only in Petrograd, but in Archangel, too, knew all about the Kitchener mission in advance. I was told at the British Boat Club that Kitchener would sail from Scapa Flow early in June and that Lloyd George was coming with him. In my opinion the Germans could not have failed to hear about this. Their Secret Service must have been very incompetent, if it didn't.' (This is the only statement which suggests that anyone outside Britain thought that Lloyd George was making the trip.)

In 1920 an emigré Russian jeweller, living in Germany, told reporters that the Czar Nicholas himself had been indirectly responsible for the Field-Marshal's end. The Czar had allegedly told a general at his Court of the invitation to Kitchener and revealed the route he was taking to Archangel. The general, who was in the pay of the German General Staff, immediately sent the information to Berlin.

Such statements are unconfirmed and must be treated with reserve. But they convey an impression of an appalling lack of security in both London and Petrograd. The Leipzig *Neuste Nachrichten*, as soon as the news of Kitchener's death was announced, claimed openly that it had known 'days in advance of the mission to Russia,' which tallies with the wireless report from Berne already mentioned. General Wetzell, Ludendorff's Chief of Staff, said that 'German intelligence circles had reports from Copenhagen, Petrograd and London which told us that Kitchener was sailing from Scapa Flow to Archangel. What action on this matter was taken, I cannot say, because even in 1925 it was considered unwise to give away our war secrets, but it can safely be assumed that some steps were taken.'

Perhaps the Russians were more to blame than the British for this laxity in security measures. Security at the Court of the Czar was almost non-existent. Nicholas himself was a weak character who had little influence on his hard-drinking and notoriously garrulous generals. He was one of those pitiful figures whose sincerity was divorced from his conduct, a dreamer of beautiful dreams who too easily forgot to live up to them, a monarch who admired British democracy intensely, yet allowed his government to perpetrate tyranny, oppression and bloodshed. But his most obvious defect was his inability to form his own judgement; it was this trait which made his generals contemptuous of him, which caused the Czarina to tell him: 'My dear Nicholas, you must not always agree with everybody. This morning M. Stolypin made a report, and after he had finished you said, "M. Stolypin, you are quite right."

'Five minutes later Durnovo came. What he told you was absolutely opposed to what Stolypin had said, but again you remarked, "My dear Durnovo, you are quite right."

"Finally, M. Schwanenbach came and told you something quite different from what the other two gentlemen had said, and again you replied, "M. Schwanenbach, you are quite right".'

To which the Czar replied: 'My dear Alexandra, you are quite right."*

Undoubtedly he was too complacent to banish from the Court that *moujik* monk, Grigori Yefimovich Rasputin. But little attention should be paid to the stories that Kitchener was betrayed to the Germans by this bogus psychiatrist. Rasputin, sinister as he may have been, was never the anti-Christ portrayed by his detractors, but he was a most convenient scapegoat. The nobles at Court disliked him because he was a *moujik* and to try to get rid of him they invented malicious stories about him. One of these was that he had been an agent of the Germans for years. There is no proof of this any more than there is the slightest iota of evidence of many of his other alleged crimes.

Aron Simonovitch, who was secretary to Rasputin and his adviser on financial and political matters, had this to say about

Prophets, Priests and Kings, by A. G. Gardiner.

Rasputin's knowledge of the events surrounding the sinking of the *Hampshire*:

'Rasputin told me he had had a talk with Nicholas II. He (Nicholas) told Rasputin that he was informed of Kitchener's departure by a secret telegram. That morning he saw only the Palace Commandant Voyekoff and Admiral Niloff. He lunched with them and at lunch a good deal was drunk.

' "Ah, I see," said Rasputin to the Czar, "so you were drunk and told your friends about the telegram. Voyekoff then blabbed it to the German spy, Andronikoff, and he in his turn informed the Germans."

'The Czar inquired of Voyekoff, who confessed that he had actually passed on to Prince Andronikoff the news which he had received from the Czar.'

All this is debatable and Simonovitch gives an impression of vagueness in his narrative which is, at the best, based on third-hand information. Other sources say it was the Tsaritsa who informed Rasputin of Kitchener's death and hinted that he had been betrayed and that, on the strength of this, the *staretz* confronted the Czar with this intelligence and demanded an explanation. But if there was a betrayal, it must have occurred about the middle of May and not, as Simonovitch would seem to suggest, after the Field-Marshal had sailed. This discrepancy may be due to faulty translation, or to a misunderstanding by Simonovitch of what Rasputin had told him.

It was not Rasputin who was the fatal cancer in the life of the Court, but the courtiers themselves. Corrupt, irresponsible, drunken and medieval, they were utterly incapable of facing up to a major war. While the ill-armed, poorly-clad, harshly treated Russian armies bled to death on the eastern front, they were rarely sober and made the Court itself a remote harlequinade. The Germans had no need of Rasputin to glean the titbits of military intelligence that spluttered and stuttered from the lips of dipsomaniacs and playboys.

* * * * *

Kitchener's state of mind at this time reflected an instinctive fear that tragedy of some sort lay ahead. Worn out with the strain and responsibilities of office, deeply hurt by the increasing intrigues against him, he was ageing visibly.

'We have to stick it out and do our very best until the release comes,' he had written to Lady Desborough. 'I only wish I could do more, or rather, that what I do was better work.'

As War Minister he worked longer hours than most of his colleagues, and, never fond of social life, he tended to rely increasingly on his own judgement and to depend less on his subordinates. It is not true to suggest that he was an innocent soldier in the midst of a pack of political wolves, who could defeat him by their subtleties. Kitchener was always more than a match for his political enemies. He had revealed his toughness and ability to get his own way years before in his tussles with the formidable Curzon, when the latter was Viceroy of India. He possessed a peculiar subtlety which was not evident on the surface; it showed itself in his knowledge that he could terrorise any subordinate likely to prove disloyal.

Today this may seem a sign of weakness, a covering up of defects, but in 1914–18, when forcefulness of character and mental toughness counted for more, it was a source of strength. Kitchener had to deal with generals who were often loyal only through fear; he used his formidable personality to create the drive necessary for winning the war. Such toughness of character was essential in dealing with generals like Sir John French and Henry Wilson.

No one could speak with such authority in the councils of the Allies as Kitchener. The volatile French, though often disagreeing with him, had a great respect for the British War Minister: it was not until after his death that they dared to dictate to the British. But without doubt the nagging feeling that he had enemies in his own Cabinet preyed heavily on a mind that was far more sensitive than was generally realised. It affected his judgement and sapped his energies.

General Sir William Robertson had not been at the War

Office as Chief of the Imperial General Staff for many days before he was urged to 'down Kitchener'. But in *From Private to Field Marshal* he made it clear that he had 'no intention of downing anyone'.

Kitchener and Robertson had an instinctive faith in each other's virtues, not in an uncritical way, but in a realisation that each possessed the qualities the other lacked. While the War Minister had authority, drive and a passion for working out details for himself, Robertson was a first-class organiser with a zest for staff work.

That the two men worked well together and had a genuine affection for each other is revealed by a remark made by Kitchener to Sir William in April 1916. 'If anything happens to me, look after Haig. Events are working up to a climax which I may not live to see. And I advise you to watch out for your own safety.'

This presentiment of death was odd in a man who had always shown a complete disregard for his own safety. Though tired, his health was sound enough, and, as far as is known, he had no reason to anticipate death from any physical cause.

His immediate aides seem to have had similar presentiments. Perhaps they suspected leakages of the mission to Russia. A letter written by Lieutenant-Colonel Fitzgerald to his family shortly before leaving London gave corroboration of these fears. 'If I do not return with my friend, you may be sure that foul play has probably been the means of our not doing so, but I hope for the best.'

Such fears cannot be dismissed as the phobias of tired minds and overwrought nerves. For a long time the War Minister's staff had had to cope with the problem of constant leakages of secret information from the War Office. It was obvious that certain politicians had been receiving confidential documents to which normally they would not be entitled. No suspicion rested on any of Kitchener's personal staff; their loyalty was unquestioned. But it undoubtedly preyed on their minds and gave rise to an atmosphere of mistrust. For the information obtained was nearly always used against Kitchener by his political opponents.

What worried the War Minister and his staff was that the leakages occurred very often before the papers and documents involved reached Kitchener. Sir Basil Thomson, chief of counter-espionage, was called in privately to investigate, but his powers were limited, because he could not trespass on the operational territory of Sir Vernon Kell, the obstinate and sometimes un-co-operative head of M.I.5.

During March and April the plot to get rid of Kitchener from the War Office took more positive shape. Bonar Law, Carson and Lloyd George were the ringleaders, but it was left to lesser figures to launch the attack. On May 31 General Sir Ivor Herbert moved the reduction of Kitchener's salary in the House of Commons. A full-scale assault on the War Minister's policies was made by Mr. Ellis Griffiths and Sir A. Markham, with the support of a few dissident Liberals. Then Mr. Tennant, on behalf of the War Office, silenced the critics by announcing that the War Minister would be glad to meet Members of Parliament and discuss the situation in private. For Kitchener, this was an untypical and quite remarkable concession to the politicians. It was as a rule difficult enough to get him to talk frankly in Cabinet meetings, let alone to back-bench M.P.s.

The meeting was held in Committee Room 14 in the House of Commons on Friday, June 2. According to Asquith whom he saw immediately afterwards, Kitchener made a 'profound impression' and 'completely carried his audience with him. . . . He left the room, gay, alert, elastic and sanguine'.

Those close to Kitchener in these last days of his life confirmed that between this meeting and his actual departure from London he was in better form and more relaxed than he had been for some time. He was in a jovial mood when he talked with a small group of trade union leaders, whom he told that he wished 'higher placed politicians could keep secrets as well as the representatives of organised labour'.

Even unpleasant news did not seem to upset him unduly

this Friday. He was told that a Canadian company in which he had shares had been given a contract for munitions by Lloyd George's Ministry, and, what was more disturbing, that Lloyd George had been gossiping about it in a sneering fashion to the press lords. There could be only one deduction as to what Lloyd George's purpose was.

According to Arthur Hodges,* Kitchener immediately gave orders to his solicitors to sell the shares at once and so absolve him from any accusation of dabbling in armament profits. Afterwards he commented to Major Humphrey Leggett: 'It is odd that a Cabinet Minister can spare the time to find out what shares other people hold. But perhaps it is a peculiar Welsh hobby.'

*Lord Kitchener (1936).

8

Espionage in a Turkish Bath

ABOUT ten days before the *Hampshire* sailed from Scapa Flow two men had a rendezvous in a Turkish baths establishment just off the Strand.

Though an unostentatious, rather austerely appointed honeycomb of rooms in a basement, it was patronised by many people well known in West End society. Ostensibly these premises were used for 'baths, massage and special treatment', but while such services were readily available, the real nature of the establishment was a place of assignation for those who wished to while away a few hours in less innocent relaxation. For years it had been one of the most discreetly run 'vice parlours' in London.

Perhaps because of this, but equally because it was frequented by influential foreigners, the Special Branch at Scotland Yard took an interest in this Turkish bath. Much valuable information was to be obtained from the clientèle, and so it became politic in war-time to tolerate its abuses. Sir Basil Thomson, whose chief concern was to maintain a close watch on all aliens, sent one of his best women agents to take a post as receptionist at the baths.

The two men entered the premises separately, one about a quarter of an hour before the other. The receptionist recognised the first man as a suspected fellow conspirator of Sir Roger Casement, who was then under arrest on a charge of treason.

The second man she did not know, but noting that he went into a cubicle adjoining that of the first visitor, she decided to keep watch and listen to their conversation.

It was not difficult to do this. She had a private cubicle of her own, cunningly concealed, with air-vents in each wall, which enabled her to listen into conversations in the massage room and other cubicles.

Her suspicions were soon confirmed. She heard a door open and close as one man went into the cubicle of the other. Then:

'Mr. Darlington's coming back and there are some very worried people over here.'

'You know that for sure?'

'Quite certain. He knows too much. And so he will get off lightly. They are too much afraid of what he may say.'

'Hm! No means of contact, I suppose.'

'With Darlington—no. Anyhow, we are much too occupied at the moment. In fact, I've just time for a shower and then I must go. Tell the boys not to be around when Mr. Darlington gets to Liverpool. Say he's got a bad cold and they might catch it. But they mustn't lose sight of the Big Fellow. Not for a minute. There's a big party on early next month. Can't say exactly when, but between the first and the tenth, and the Big Fellow is the chief guest.'

'A champagne party?'

'No, old chap, much stronger stuff. You know how it is at these new parties. They prefer spirits—vodka, stuff like that.'

'Where is it being held?'

'Your guess is as good as mine. But they'll probably start off at Florence's.'

'I see. I suppose we can make it.'

'You'd better.'

*   *   *   *   *

Such cryptic exchanges of pleasantry would have been lost on most eavesdroppers. Not so on Sir Basil Thomson's agent. Her keen brain had concentrated the moment she heard the phrase 'Mr. Darlington', for this had been a pseudonym used in the intelligence world for Trebitsch Lincoln, the renegade M.P. Very careless, she thought, for anyone to use this name. It suggested the speaker was a double-agent.

Another error had been made. 'Florence's' was an enemy code-name for Scapa Flow. Although she might have been mistaken about this, it hardly seemed likely that this was mere coincidence. The trend of the talk suggested it had a *double entendre*. Like all good agents she made no attempt to write down what she had heard, but kept repeating the phrases, memorising them and trying to sort out the puzzle.

If Darlington was Trebitsch Lincoln, then how did Liverpool come into it? Lincoln was in New York. Then slowly she realised what was happening. Lincoln was being arrested and brought back to Liverpool and somebody must keep away from there and avoid being seen when he returned. Doubtless the British intelligence expected somebody to try to contact Lincoln, or signal to him as he stepped ashore.

If 'Florence' was Scapa Flow, then the party must be a naval operation. That seemed certain. But at that point the woman agent was baffled. She reported what she had heard to Sir Basil Thomson, who listened in grim silence for a long time, then interrupted her with:

'You are getting tired. It often happens. Too much work, too vivid an imagination. And then the agent becomes not an asset but a damned liability. Take a rest. I'll see you have a change in the near future.'

'But I am quite sure this is something important.'

'Yes, I dare say you are so tensed up that any scrap of conversation seems important. But it isn't. And you'll forget it. Forget it fast before your mind gets cluttered up with other unnecessary details. The man you seem so convinced is a spy is in fact one of our own counter-espionage agents. Normally I wouldn't tell you this. Against the rules. But it's as well you should know before you make a fool of yourself again.'

The woman agent was annoyed. After all she had been 'in

the game' for some years. She had handled quite tough assignments calling for initiative and sound judgement. Why should she be disbelieved now?

'Have I ever let you down?' she inquired.

'Don't argue.'

'I refuse to be silenced like this. You are treating me as though I'm a child.'

'Listen, woman. If you don't keep silent, I'll find means of forcing you to be quiet.'

Angry, bewildered and baffled by Sir Basil's attitude, she shrugged her shoulders, politely but coldly said 'Good day', and flounced out of his office.

* * * * *

The account of these conversations is set down as it was given to me by the woman agent, Madame Hubert. In her late seventies, still mentally alert and with a retentive memory, she lives in Lisbon, the widow of a Swiss hotelier whom she married after the First World War.

When the news of Lord Kitchener's death was announced she recalled the strange conversation in the Turkish baths. She knew this establishment was used by suspected enemy agents—one had been arrested as a result of a visit there—and she felt sure that what she had heard had some significance.

'It dawned on me quite suddenly who the counter-espionage agent Sir Basil had mentioned was. I had not seen him before, but I described him to a masseur at the baths. "Oh, yes, I know who you mean," he said. "He's an Irish lawyer."

'I tried to see Sir Basil Thomson again. He refused to see me. Shortly afterwards I was "relieved" of my post at the Turkish baths. I used this as excuse to seek an interview with Sir Basil, but instead was seen by some minor intelligence officer who completely pooh-poohed my story. I suppose I was impetuous and should not have crossed swords with Sir Basil on this issue. He was a most brilliant intelligence chief, but ruthless and unrelenting. He never forgave anyone who challenged his authority in the slightest degree.

'It had dawned on me that "champagne" must mean France and "vodka", Russia. In that case Scapa Flow fitted into the picture, and who else could the "Big Fellow" be, but Kitchener. But I couldn't prove anything. What puzzled me was why our intelligence were so sure this Irishman was absolutely safe.

'Years later I met Arthur Maundy Gregory, the man who was jailed for selling honours. He had been a neighbour of mine in Albion Street, Bayswater, during the war, and I always understood that he did some sort of intelligence work. He was a mysterious character, so much so that it was almost eerie talking to him. But he had immense charm and, though not a woman's man, he understood women perfectly and made himself most agreeable to them. I mentioned this story to him.

'Gregory was in a pretty affluent state at this time. He asked me out to lunch and cross-examined me on my account of what had happened at the Turkish baths.

'Then, smiling that odd, slow, enigmatic smile of his, he casually remarked: "Yes, you very nearly stumbled on one of the scandals of the war. Your deduction wasn't far off the mark. About Trebitsch Lincoln I know nothing; I do not think that part of your story is important.

' "But the 'big party' was certainly the Kitchener Mission to Moscow. You see, at that time, there were two plots against Kitchener, both of them Irish in origin. The first was to defame him by forging a scurrilous document containing allegations of homosexuality.

' "The Irish planned to plant this document on somebody with a view to discrediting Kitchener and bringing about his disgrace. It was a pack of lies, but, by having Kitchener watched and followed, they aimed to produce a document that should be unassailable as far as places and dates were concerned.

' "If Kitchener went down to Broome in Kent, then the date and times were noted, but fictitious reports of what he did and whom he saw would be written. Kitchener's death prevented the report being used in Britain, but it was smuggled out to Germany where distorted versions of it were used by enemy agents. With Kitchener dead, it wasn't much good to anybody; but it left a nasty smear on a great man.

' "I am one of the few men now living who have read the original Casement Diaries from beginning to end, and the Irish fantasy on Kitchener. I will say nothing about the former, but the latter was a tissue of lies. It could have done immense harm and produced a national scandal greater than that of the Casement Diaries."

'I suggested to Maundy Gregory that, as he was a personal friend of Sir Basil Thomson, he might repeat to him what he had told me. He said he would so so.

'Years passed by and I neither heard nor saw anything of Gregory until I read about his going to jail when he was found guilty of trying to sell honours. When he came out of jail he went to live in Paris and in 1933 I met him in the Hotel Meurice in that city. Once again I brought up the subject of the conversation I had overheard in the Turkish baths. Had he ever seen Sir Basil Thomson again, I asked, and had he mentioned to him the matter we had discussed.

'He said he was sorry, but that he had forgotten all about it. However, as Sir Basil was now living in Normandy he sometimes saw him. In fact, he was going to see him the following week and he would make a point of raising the subject. Indeed, possibly he could arrange a lunch at which I could meet Sir Basil.

'To my surprise a week or two later I received a charming letter from Sir Basil in which he said that he had met Gregory and had been most interested to have news of me. Could I lunch with him in Paris in the near future?

'In due course I lunched with Basil Thomson and Gregory. The former couldn't have been more agreeable. He apologised for what might have seemed churlishness on his part during the war, but he assured me there were good reasons for his attitude then.

' "I knew all about the attempts to smear Kitchener's character and the Irishman you saw had been detailed by us to trap those who were compiling the false dossier. I couldn't tell you that because it was essential that as few people as possible knew what was going on. Unfortunately the Irishman turned out to be a double-agent and we never caught the plotters. I wish now that I had listened to you." '

Madame Hubert was, however, convinced that she had not been told the whole story. Both Thomson and Gregory were evasive when it came to details. She asked Gregory what was the 'second plot' against Kitchener which he had mentioned when they met before. On this subject he was less forthcoming, but he hinted that the Irish Republican Army had sworn to kill the War Minister and that he had no doubt that the Irishman in the Turkish baths was an I.R.A., if not a German, agent.

Maundy Gregory was not the type of man whose evidence can be accepted without a great deal of reservation. Though supposed to have been an intelligence agent for Britain, he was a notorious liar and romancer. In the days of his exile in France he boasted of his links with the Secret Service and told visitors that one of the two telephones he had in his flat in the Rue d'Anjou was 'a direct line to Scotland Yard'. Sir Basil Thomson himself had no official connections with Scotland Yard then and was in retirement.

Two years later Mme. Hubert received this letter from Maundy Gregory: 'I have seen Thomson again and we talked about the events of long ago. Without question you came across some valuable evidence that day in the Turkish baths, though it was not appreciated at the time. However, it is exceedingly doubtful whether that evidence could have prevented the

Hampshire tragedy unless, of course, it had caused the port of departure to be changed.

'I see there has been more controversy about the Casement Diaries. I am an old man and probably can expect only a few years more of this life, but I think it is as well to record a few useful observations before I pass on. Whatever are the rights or the wrongs of the Casement Diaries, whether they were doctored, or whether they were genuine, is beside the point. I have my own views. But the Irish can hardly claim to be angels.

'It may well be that our own authorities were too pre-occupied with tracking down the authors of the disgusting fictional report on Lord Kitchener to be able to notice an even deadlier plot. What is certain is that if the Casement Diaries were forged, and I do not say they were, most definitely the Kitchener Dossier was a damnable piece of criminal libel, deliberately concocted without an iota of evidence to blacken the character of the War Minister and force him out of office.

'There was an attempt to sell that document to a British Cabinet Minister, one whom the Irish knew wanted Kitchener out of the way. In that fact you have the clue to how the Irish hoped to succeed. Terrible as it is to say so, perhaps Kitchener's end coming as it did was a blessing in disguise, for assuredly the knowledge of this plot would have killed him even if it had been disproved. It is so very easy to blacken a man's character.'

*   *   *   *   *

During the weekend before Kitchener left for Thurso a review of all persons suspected of having designs on Kitchener's life was carried out by Sir Basil Thomson. This was a considerable task as for many years there had been attempts to kill Kitchener in various parts of the world. A network of plots against him had been discovered by the police in Egypt, and in July 1912 an attempt to shoot him was made at Cairo railway station by a well-known seditionist, Taber Arabi. Fourteen months later another plan was made to kill him on his return to England. Fortunately he had told no one of his movements and went to Pisa first, so that by the time he arrived in Venice the suspects had been rounded up.

Yet in June 1916 it was known in London that the ring-leaders in Egypt were still active and had joined forces with the Germans. The latter had long since marked down Kitchener as their principal target for assassination. In October 1915, the British counter-espionage authorities had reported to Sir Basil Thomson that the Germans had been using an Indian revolutionary named Chattopadhya for this purpose. News came from Switzerland that Chattopadhya was planning Kitchener's assassination and using as agents a young Swiss girl and a German woman both married to Indians living in Britain. The Swiss girl was detained and the others interned.

The Irish Republicans were also known to have the War Minister on their 'death list'. They had vowed to kill him because of his refusal to allow Irish troops to wear the emblem of the harp on their uniforms. This was a foolish act on Kitchener's part, for, whatever the military objections might have been, they would have been more than cancelled out by the goodwill engendered by the granting of this patriotic request.

During May the activities of the Irish Republicans regarding Kitchener gave the counter-espionage authorities most cause for concern. The last-minute security check-up, which was reported to Thomson on June 2, revealed that Republican agents were suspected of having watched the War Minister for weeks past. There seems to have been some delay in getting this report to Thomson's office—could it have been that his trusted Irish agent let him down?—and consequently it was too late to take effective action. When, belatedly, the information was passed on to Naval Intelligence, it was never acted upon for the simple reason that the N.I.D. were too busily occupied with reports of the Battle of Jutland. The full effects of this preoccupation will be seen later.

On the Saturday morning the War Minister was still at work

L.K.D.—H

in London. He went to Buckingham Palace to say good-bye to the King, with whom he lunched. Then he motored down to Broome Hall, his country home in Kent. He spent the remainder of the day rearranging his pictures and china and happily pottering about in his garden with Lieutenant-Colonel Fitzgerald and Major Humphrey Leggett, admiring his roses, of which he was justly proud.

Broome Hall was situated at Barham, midway between Canterbury and Dover. It was the house built by Inigo Jones for Sir Basil Dixwell, who signed the death warrant for Charles I, and stood in some 600 acres of park-land and gardens. Here Kitchener invariably retired at week-ends to snatch a few hours' respite from the trials of office. He had filled the Great Hall with his treasures and souvenirs of his campaigns, a rug made from the skins of twenty-four bears he had shot, suits of armour chased in silver and gold and Chinese screens from the Palace of Pekin. Here, too, he kept his collection of pictures and china. On the Saturday evening he set to work with a piece of charcoal, drawing his coat of arms on the two stone panels of a fireplace. He had just started on the words 'Beati Pacifici' when he was interrupted by the arrival of a messenger. The task was never finished.

During that last week-end at Broome one of Lord Kitchener's gardeners, a Mr. Dudeney, declared, 'The master was in excellent spirits at this time. He thoroughly enjoyed strolling round his gardens. But there was one incident which seemed to bother him. He stopped suddenly and looked around him in all directions. I asked him if anything was wrong.

' "I was just wondering how many staff I really had here," he replied. "In the last hour I have seen two men I do not know. Have you taken on additional staff?"

'I told him that the staff had been reduced owing to the call-up. I asked him to point out the two men to me. But we never saw them again, and Lord Kitchener never referred to the matter after that. But when I mentioned it to Lieutenant-Colonel Fitzgerald, he was very perturbed and angry. He told me I should have reported it to him before. "This isn't the first time we have been watched by two strange men in the last few weeks," he said.'

On Sunday Kitchener's spirits seemed to droop again. 'Something was obviously worrying him, and I couldn't help noticing it because he had been so cheerful before. He became moody after a messenger called at the Hall with a dispatch.

'Then, just before he went back to York House on Sunday, he made a very odd remark to me as he said good-bye. "Look after the roses, Dudeney," he said. "See that no strange people try to *assassinate* them." '

* * * * *

In April 1926 an article on the subject of Lord Kitchener's death appeared in the *Daily Express*. Its author was Mr. A. C. Fox-Davies, a barrister-at-law who had served in the Naval Law branch of the Admiralty.

The article contained this admission 'It was known in Fleet Street eight days beforehand that the *Hampshire* was detailed to take Lord Kitchener to Russia.'

Now Mr. Fox-Davies would hardly be likely to make a statement like this on hearsay. It was during the period that he served at the Admiralty that the *Hampshire* was lost, and, as he himself explained 'An Allied Government sometime later asked for details. I made the précis which was sent in reply and for that purpose I had through my hands every single paper the Admiralty possessed about the matter.'

Mr. Fox-Davies' statement that Fleet Street knew all about the mission to Russia is confirmed from various sources. The news was known by Northcliffe and Lord Riddell, proprietor of the *News of the World*. Thomas Marlow, editor of the *Daily Mail*, had heard of it; so, too, had Mr. Robert Donald, of the *Daily Chronicle*. But how the press came to hear of this supposedly top secret information is far from clear. Thomas Marlow might have heard from Lord Northcliffe, or even, in confidence, from Admiral Sir Reginald Hall, Chief of Naval

Intelligence, who was his close friend and with whom he co-operated on occasions in naval counter-espionage. Yet it is almost unthinkable that Hall would have passed on news about the *Hampshire* even to so trusted a colleague.

Northcliffe had one friend only in the Cabinet at this time—Lloyd George. As many improper disclosures of Cabinet discussions were passed on to Northcliffe by Lloyd George, it is possible that the latter was the purveyor of the information about Kitchener's mission. Years afterwards Lord Riddell, after he had quarrelled with Lloyd George, told Lord Dalziel 'Lloyd George had a presentiment about the *Hampshire*. About a week before it sailed he told me that Kitchener was going in this ship and that he was glad he wasn't sailing in such an old tub.'

On November 5, 1915, the *Globe* published a statement that Lord Kitchener had tendered his resignation to the King when in fact he was about to leave the country on a secret mission. In his book *Queer People* Sir Basil Thomson stated that this was the only daily newspaper to be suppressed during the war, on account of the publication of this false news.

'That information,' said Mr. J. W. Gibbons, a journalist who worked on the *Globe*, 'came from Lloyd George himself. But he afterwards denied having said anything of the sort, arguing that he had merely hinted that there was talk of Kitchener resigning.'

British newspapers were not alone in receiving news of the 1916 Russian mission. Apart from the *Neuste Nachrichten* of Leipzig, whose editor claimed he had ordered an obituary notice of Kitchener to be set up in type three days beforehand on the strength of the information, the Paris office of the *New York Times* also had a tip. That newspaper's correspondent in Paris, Wythe Williams, had it from two sources—from a Northcliffe contact in London and from a member of the Russian arms purchasing mission to America.

'I made no use of the information,' said Wythe Williams. 'It was obviously too hot for a friendly neutral nation to pass on. In any case it would never have got through the French censorship. But I was assured from London that Lloyd George and Kitchener were going to Russia together and sailing in the first week of June.

'I did not know the name of the ship in which they were supposed to be travelling, but my Russian contact assured me they were expected in Archangel about June 10. He added that the decision to send Lloyd George appeared to have been kept secret from the Russian authorities because officially Petrograd had no intimation that he would be paying a visit. He assumed that the British were afraid that Russia might oppose the inclusion of Lloyd George in the mission.'

There is no reason to doubt that Wythe Williams' informant was accurately describing what he had been told, for this Russian officer continued for more than thirty years to keep Williams well informed on European affairs. In the nineteen-thirties and early 'forties Williams edited a small, though widely read suburban newspaper, *Greenwich Time*, in Connecticut. Through this medium he kept readers more closely informed of developments inside Germany than any other newspaper in the world. Admiringly, Lowell Thomas wrote: 'From his desk in Greenwich Wythe Williams proceeded to pull one news rabbit after another out of his hat. He had us . . . not only guessing, but more than slightly sceptical. How could one man, we asked, dig up information not available to the great American wire services, to say nothing of the great newspapers who had their own news gathering machinery in addition?'

Modestly, Wythe Williams, though he had many contacts, attributed his major scoops to one man—the former Russian Army officer, to whom, in his book *Secret Sources*, he gave the pseudonym of 'van Narvig'.

One might regard 'van Narvig' as a mythical character, but the information he passed on to Wythe Williams during World War II was so detailed and accurate that it could only have come from someone who was working in Hitler's entourage. In World War I, according to Williams, he had played much the same role, often pretending to be a German agent. He claimed he had received the news of the Kitchener mission from a German agent who obtained it 'in a Turkish baths establishment in London'.

This is not the only piece of evidence which links up with Madame Hubert's story. Shortly after the Nazis came to power Colonel Walther Nicolai, Germany's intelligence chief, was asked officially to investigate all dossiers on the loss of the *Hampshire*. When he asked what was the object of this investigation, he was sharply rebuffed and told it was not his concern.

Herr Otto Stoermer, a former *Abwehr* officer, and a confidant of Colonel Nicolai, told me: 'Colonel Nicolai was not very popular in his last years and he did not always have the confidence of the authorities. He felt this keenly. But it made it very difficult to investigate a subject when we had no idea what we were meant to look for.

'Obviously, nobody would want a re-hash of the Naval dossiers, which were very detailed. So we concentrated instead on our own intelligence reports received during the month before the *Hampshire* sailed.

'Reports from London, Copenhagen and Petrograd told us all about the proposed Russian mission. The news we had from Petrograd was due to poor security by the Russians and British. But the information we had from Copenhagen and London, which tallied in every respect, came from agents who had no contact with one another. But they got their intelligence from the same source. That source was a contact in a Turkish baths off the Strand in London, somebody who was close to the Lloyd George circle.

'At first we suspected the information because of its source and we felt sure it had been deliberately planted to mislead us. But the news from Petrograd gave us all the confirmation we required.'

While none of this evidence is conclusive, it certainly suggests that there was appalling carelessness, which allowed news of the mission to leak out. The main puzzle is why Lloyd

George told so many different stories about the mission. What was the purpose of his telling people right up to the last moment that he was going to Russia, when it was quite certain that he was not to be a member of the party? Why, at the same period, should he tell Riddell alone that he was 'glad he was not going'?

Lloyd George was guilty of various indiscretions during the war, divulging confidential information to people not entitled to it. But he was not in the habit of doing this without a purpose. Trained as a lawyer, he could keep a secret as well as any man when he wished. What could have been his reason for informing the press about Kitchener's movements and the false story (perpetuated by his biographers) that he himself was bound for Russia? He knew that secrecy was essential for the safety of the Secretary of State for War in that most vital mission—nothing less than an attempt to stave off collapse in Czarist Russia. Probably Lloyd George's motives in the political activities which preceded the mission to Russia will for ever remain an enigma. All that seems certain is that he did divulge the information to certain people. For two years Lloyd George had been intriguing against the War Minister. Leakages of Cabinet business aimed at discrediting Kitchener and Asquith had been continually occurring. Mrs. Asquith noted in her diary 'When I point out that someone in the Cabinet is betraying secrets, I am counselled to keep calm. Henry is as indifferent to the press as St. Paul's Cathedral is to midges, but I confess that I am not, and I can only hope that the man responsible for giving information to Lord N—— will be heavily punished. God may forgive him: I never can.'

The news of Kitchener's death had hardly been received before Lloyd George was plotting to succeed him. An inspired paragraph in *The Times* of June 12 said that the new War Minister would 'almost certainly be Mr. Lloyd George'.

Dr. Erwin Weiss, Director of the World War Library at Stuttgart, and a most conscientious researcher, makes these observations in a letter to me:

'The problem which you are working on has personally interested me myself and I have taken the opportunity to consult with various historians.

'From a conversation with the then Chief of Defence, Colonel Nicolai, in the year 1937, I believe that the conclusion can be drawn that the German intelligence received advance news of the journey of Lord Kitchener to Russia.

'I am of the opinion that various circles in Britain had a certain interest in desiring Lord Kitchener's disappearance from active politics. Whether it is right that the sinking of the *Hampshire* can be traced to plots of the Irish-Freedom fighters I would not venture to decide.

'That forces in Britain, not well disposed to Kitchener, were in some way at work seems proved in that right up to now it has not been possible to see the reports of the British Admiralty (including the secret reports). The British Admiralty today has obviously not the slightest reason for keeping secret either a Russian or a German act of sabotage.

'The key to the puzzle must lie with the people who wished, as a matter of internal policy, to prevent Lord Kitchener, in view of his popularity, from achieving a position of power which they in no circumstances desired.

'Perhaps in this the antagonism of Lloyd George to the War Minister played a certain role.

'I believe that it can be taken as certain that the solution of the riddle can only be evolved in Britain itself.

'It must be understood that the opinions that I have expressed are absolutely personal. Nearly twenty years have passed since I occupied myself with this case. On the basis of my experience at that time I believe the above conclusions can be drawn.'

There is a curious postscript to this chapter. Within a few months of Kitchener's death Lloyd George was angling for support from Bonar Law in a scheme which, say the biographers of Asquith, 'Lloyd George was hatching for a War Council with himself at the head of it, and to consider his plan for getting rid of Sir William Robertson, Chief of the Imperial General Staff, whom he considered to be a great obstacle to his schemes, by sending him on a mission to St. Petersburg.'*

Bonar Law, whose inability to make up his mind was quite incredible at times, must have scented a sinister plot, for, according to Lord Beaverbrook, he then took the view that 'in matters of office and power Lloyd George was a self-seeker and a man who considered no interests but his own'.

There is confirmation of this in Mr. Malcolm Thomson's biography of Lloyd George. 'Robertson, advised by some of Lloyd George's enemies in the Cabinet that it was a scheme to get him away from the War Office, refused to go.'

*The Life of Lord Oxford and Asquith: J. A. Spender and Cyril Asquith.

9

An Inquiry Demanded

'THE mystery which veiled a blameless soldier in the hour of storm and darkness, no less than the long and persistent disbelief in his death, belonged to the same order as the passing of King Arthur.'

So wrote Sir George Arthur, and he might have added that the various versions of events which followed the Field-Marshal's death were as mythical and unsubstantiated as the Arthurian legends.

Undeniably there was in the disaster which overtook the *Hampshire* the material from which an imaginative and dramatic thriller could be woven. But there was more to it than that. The sinking off Birsay marked a turning point in history. Kitchener's death meant that the last chance had been lost of bolstering up the Russian army and staving off the fall of the Czarist regime. It contributed, however indirectly, to the doom of the Czar and the emergence of Communist tyranny. According to some sources, the War Minister was taking with him to Russia a list of revolutionaries in Petrograd who were in the pay of Germany: from his own intelligence sources he had prepared a list which the Czarist Government would have given much to receive. And, such was the reticence of the man, the secrets contained in this list were lost with him. Had he reached Archangel, it is not impossible that the course of the war might have been changed. It is almost certain that the Asquith

Government would not have fallen the following December, for Kitchener would always have sided with Asquith (almost the only politician whom he trusted) against Lloyd George, and few Tories would have dared go against the War Minister.

There was an acute state of panic in intelligence circles after the loss of the *Hampshire* because, while it was known that Kitchener was taking important dossiers to Russia, the actual contents of these documents had not been communicated to anyone in either the Foreign Office or the War Office. It was stated in the press long afterwards that a notice had been posted up outside Kirkwall dockyard offering a reward of £100 for the recovery of Lord Kitchener's dispatch case. Despite exhaustive inquiries in Orkney today, nobody can recall having seen any such notice, or even having heard about it. Yet the Admiralty White Paper clearly states: '. . . a look out was also kept and rewards offered for documents relating to Lord Kitchener's mission which might possibly float ashore in dispatch cases or the like.'

Demands for an inquiry into the sinking of the *Hampshire* were swiftly made, and M.P.s were not satisfied by the Admiralty's promptness in ordering an investigation. What worried M.P.s were the published hints that news of the mission had leaked to the enemy.

Commander Bellairs and Sir Richard Cooper both questioned Dr. MacNamara, the Admiralty spokesman in the House of Commons, and asked for a court martial. Dr. MacNamara replied that he did 'not propose to hold another inquiry' and that it was 'not considered necessary to have a court martial'.

At so early a stage he could hardly have been expected to reply otherwise, for who, other than the Commander-in-Chief, could have been court-martialled?

On June 22, 1916, Sir Henry Dalziel asked: 'Has the Right Honourable Gentleman any information to the effect that a vessel flying the Dutch flag was discerned immediately before the *Hampshire* reached the spot where she went down? Is there a suspicion that she was a minelayer?'

The reply was: 'I have no information.'

On July 6 Sir Richard Cooper again urged that there should be a court martial in view of the 'disagreement among the survivors' as to what actually happened. He spoke of rumours that the bodies of survivors showed traces of having been 'burned by acids' and that one survivor was under arrest.

Dr. MacNamara's answer was hardly reassuring: 'I do not deny that there may have been espionage, but I think it is unlikely.'

Outside Parliament the wildest rumours continued to circulate, but, as it was war-time, there was little opportunity of ventilating them. It was after the war that the demand for a public inquiry gained momentum both inside and outside Parliament.

In 1922 the Sun Publishing Company of Vancouver produced a book entitled *The Message: Lord Kitchener Lives*, which claimed to be the revelations of the dead Field-Marshal made through a spiritualist medium, Ala Mana, to Margaret Mabel O'Brien. Spiritualism became a popular cult in the years immediately after World War I, and this book was but one of many which sought to propagate the cult. A few brief extracts from *The Message* will suffice to show how wildly fantastic and inaccurate it was. Describing the scene, as the *Hampshire* steamed towards Birsay, the authoress wrote: 'It was rather foggy': it was not, of course, anything of the sort.

She made the spirit of Kitchener say: 'I was attracted to a cabin boy who darted in the shadows . . . submarines were following us for hours . . . I heard the key click in the cabin door. I pulled out my watch as I stepped towards the door. It was about 8.45.'

Apart from the fact that H.M. ships do not have cabin boys and that Kitchener would not have erred in describing even a Boy Second Class in such terms, by 8.45 p.m. the *Hampshire* had gone to the bottom.

There followed a description of how Kitchener tried to open the door, but found it had been locked by the cabin boy who afterwards 'shot himself', presumably in remorse!

Over the years vague reports appeared in the world's press that Kitchener had been seen alive in some distant part. In March 1917, a crofter's wife, walking home along the cliff top near Birsay, ran to the police and claimed she had actually seen Lord Kitchener alive. She took the police to a cave in the cliffs and indicated where she had seen him—'alone, staggering along and trying to signal to me'.

Needless to say, nothing or nobody was found. This was just another example of the association of ideas, for when the police made inquiries they learned of the story of the 'Ghost of Black Craigs'. On March 5, 1834, during a storm, a schooner, *The Star of Dundee*, drifted helplessly on to the rocks of Black Craigs, not far from Stromness. Days later, when it was assumed that all lives had been lost, a man was seen on top of the cliffs. He was the sole survivor. He had been washed into a cave and miraculously saved. But the islanders swore he was a ghost. Somehow the legend had survived and doubtless was resuscitated after the loss of the *Hampshire*.

Pathos gave way to bathos and for some few years there was a profusion of speeches, books, articles, pamphlets and letters to the press expressing a diversity of theories, hallucinations and more often impudently disguised fiction about what really happened on that June evening in 1916.

On December 23, 1925, Captain Waterhouse, M.P., asked the First Lord of the Admiralty whether he was in a position to give any fresh information as to the circumstances in which the loss of the *Hampshire* occurred.

In a written reply the First Lord, Mr. Bridgeman, stated: 'It is not a fact that the sailing of the *Hampshire* was an open secret. She was not selected by the Commander-in-Chief for this service until May 27, ten days before she sailed to Russia. She was engaged in the Battle of Jutland from May 30 to June 2.'

This date—May 27—may or may not be correct. According to Admiral Sir Henry Oliver, who made the sailing arrangements, the decision to use the *Hampshire* for the mission was made as early as May 18 and was confirmed officially on May 23. There seems to have been no question of selecting another ship in reserve in case the *Hampshire* did not return to base by June 5. Probably the C.-in-C. was never informed that the cruiser had been chosen for the Russian mission and the Admiralty did not know that the C.-in-C. was planning to send her out with the Grand Fleet.

Mr. Bridgeman was more categorical than any other First Lord had been. 'The Admiralty have no doubt whatever that H.M.S. *Hampshire* struck a mine laid by the U.75, a mine-laying submarine which had been sent out to watch the Orkneys and to lay mines in preparation for the German sortie which resulted in the Battle of Jutland.'

The First Lord continued: 'the Admiralty have followed their usual course of not publishing Court of Inquiry proceedings. It is absolutely untrue that the Admiralty have held back important papers that would throw a new light upon this disaster, and I may add that the allegation that spies had on a former occasion been found in the *Hampshire* and shot is a ridiculous and wicked fabrication.'

Sir Richard Cooper was as assiduous in pressing the demand for an inquiry in 1926 as he had been ten years earlier. In a letter to the *Daily Telegraph* on January 5, 1926, he declared: 'This tragedy is not the sport of a few cranks. A vast number of people felt at the time that there was something radically wrong with the arrangements under which Lord Kitchener sailed from the Orkneys for Russia.

'This mainly arose from the fact that the two destroyers which accompanied the *Hampshire* returned a few minutes after setting sail,* on account of the state of the weather, leaving this man-of-war to make the journey alone and unprotected at the certain mercy both of mines and submarines,

*This is, of course, inaccurate.

which everyone knew to be infesting the North Sea, six months after the intensive submarine warfare had been in progress.

'The recent statement of the First Lord compels me to return to the subject, because some of his statements are opposed to the facts. . . . He says "It is absolutely untrue that the Admiralty have held back important papers which would throw a new light on this disaster." The Admiralty published the first report from the Commander-in-Chief at Scapa Flow. They have held back the second report in face of the most responsible application for a sight of it; indeed, they have offered to permit a perusal of it under strict promise that not a word of it shall be divulged to anyone.

'If it was right for the public to be given the first report, the public are entitled to the second report, and until it is made public I hold that there is every justification for suspicion and anxiety.

'Again, the First Lord says: ". . . the allegation that spies had on a former occasion been found in the *Hampshire* and had been shot is a ridiculous and wicked fabrication." The fact is that on a former occasion spies had been found in the *Hampshire* and had been shot. The case which occurred at Belfast, when the ship was undergoing repairs, was raised by me at the time, and was dropped when my statement in the House of Commons was confirmed by the Admiralty. I hope the First Lord will at once insist on having the facts of the two cases I cite placed before him.'

This allegation about spies having been found on the cruiser and afterwards shot was mentioned in articles in the press as well as in the House of Commons. Sir Richard Cooper insisted that his own story was admitted in private by the Admiralty; it was said that the spy story was vouched for by one of the survivors (whose name could not be divulged because 'he might be persecuted') and confirmed in a declaration by the editor of the *Belfast News*.

Mr. Frank Power wrote in the *Sunday Referee*: 'The survivor referred to, who must not be allowed to run the risk of penalisation by the publishing of his name at the moment, writes to me as follows:

' "In the early part of 1916, while the ship was being refitted at the yard at Belfast,* half the ship's company were on leave. It was about 3.30 in the afternoon when I came out of the engine room and when I came on deck I found that the ship was surrounded with soldiers.

' "I inquired what was wrong, and was told that someone had been tampering with the electric switches in the ammunition passage and that no one was allowed to leave the ship. The soldiers stood with fixed bayonets and two of the ship's company were at the gangway to identify a certain man (or men) who had been seen lingering about the ammunition passage.

' "This man, I was told by my messmate, was dressed in overalls, the same as the shipyard workers. My messmate's name was F——, stoker. Later we learned that two men had been shot in the barracks ashore.' "

The publication of Sir George Arthur's letter in *The Times*, when he raised the question of the existence of a secret report, led to another spate of questions in the Commons. Mr. Bridgeman was confronted not only by Sir Robert Hamilton (Liberal Member for Orkney and Zetland) and Mr. Patrick Hannon (Conservative Member for Moseley), but by Mr. Scrymgeour (Labour M.P. for Dundee).

In replying to questions from these three M.P.s, the First Lord said: 'That Lord Long, as First Lord of the Admiralty, offered in 1920 to show the report in confidence to Lord Kitchener's former secretary, Sir George Arthur, is, I believe, a fact, but it does not detract from the importance attached to the inviolability of such reports.'

Sir Robert Hamilton declined to be put off by this statement and fired this broadside at the now harassed Mr. Bridgeman: 'Is the First Lord aware that the answer he has just given is directly contradictory to the one given the previous week, when

*This refit took place in February, 1916.

he said that the Admiralty had published *all* the information at their disposal. Having regard to what he has now said, will he further consider the question of publishing all the information?'

Mr. Bridgeman then insisted that it had never been stated that the full report of the Naval Inquiry was published. This was a quibble, for in repeated statements the Admiralty spokesmen in the Commons had given the firm impression that all essential facts had been published.

On another occasion, when Mr. Scrymgeour returned to the attack by asking whether the Admiralty would be 'prepared to receive the evidence of the *fifteen* survivors', he was blithely informed that the evidence of 'all these survivors was already in the possession of the Admiralty'.

It was not until Commander Fanshawe (Conservative Member for Clackmannan and a member of the original Court of Inquiry) intervened to point out that there were only twelve survivors that the Admiralty spokesman hastened blushingly to agree with him.

Mr. Scrymgeour's question was prompted by statements in the press suggesting that there had been fifteen survivors, three of whom had been 'spirited away'.

Other questions were asked in Parliament about the existence of a secret report. This time the Home Secretary, Sir William Joynson Hicks, was the target of the questioners. He was asked by Major R. I. Tasker, Conservative M.P. for East Islington, 'whether he would consider the desirability of issuing a report made by a Scotland Yard official in reference to the sinking of H.M.S. *Hampshire*.'

The Home Secretary bluntly replied that there was 'no report'. Another member who inquired further into the matter was asked to the Table of the House of Commons and told his questions could not be put as 'no Minister is responsible for it'.

Now, if such an inquiry had been made on behalf of the Secret Service, no departmental Minister would be responsible, but it was quite unconstitutional to suggest that no member of His Majesty's Government could be called to account. If this had been a matter for the Secret Service, then the Prime Minister, as its political chief, was clearly responsible. But Major Tasker's error was in referring the question to the Home Secretary. No inquiry was made, as far as is known, under Home Office instructions, so it was quite simple for an official denial of such a report to be made.

Unfortunately, Members of Parliament do not always take care to make sure of all their facts before they put questions. For example, Mr. Bridgeman was subsequently asked about the reports of a 'Lieutenant Vance' to the Admiral Commanding Orkney and Shetland.

'They cannot be traced,' replied the First Lord complacently. And he declined to interview 'Lieutenant Vance'.

Naturally—for 'Lieutenant Vance' did not exist. The questioner had only got half the story.

*   *   *   *   *

This year—1926—was a critical period for Britain. It was an era of mass unemployment, of widespread poverty and social decay, of hardship in tens of thousands of homes, of strife among the organised workers and a deep sense of frustration and resentment at the failure of successive governments to produce Lloyd George's 'land fit for heroes to live in'.

Yet the Members of Parliament who might have been pressing the drifting and shifting Baldwin Government to take action in the coalfields, were often more concerned at solving the mystery of the *Hampshire*. This was no red herring trailed to embarrass the Government; for after all, the Baldwin Government was in no way responsible for what took place in 1916; and most of the members who raised the subject so irately were not opponents of the Government, but Tory backbenchers. But it is one of the strengths as well as one of the weaknesses of democracy that M.P.s, once convinced that somebody is hiding something, will, regardless of party ties, press for the truth to be told, however remote, frivolous or even unimportant the issue.

It was the Government which, quite unnecessarily, embarrassed itself. The evasions, the testiness and off-handedness of Ministers, the complete lack of candour on the part of the First Lord, prolonged this rather futile verbal duelling. Most of the questions asked were badly phrased, based on erratic judgement and rumour. It was easy to shoot them down. But the First Lord and others might have been dairy maids on a grouse moor, so ham-handed and furtive was their approach.

The newspapers joined the demand for a publication of all the facts. And no fewer than seventy-eight branches of the British Legion in all parts of the country passed resolutions calling for a full inquiry.

Echoes of the *Hampshire* disaster came from Germany. The fumbling of Ministers and the agitation of the British people for the whole truth prompted some Germans to make the episode into a national espionage triumph. It was said in Berlin that a woman spy had been directly responsible for Kitchener's death. General Ludendorff, rather cryptically, wrote: 'Kitchener's mysterious death was the work neither of a German mine nor torpedo, but of that power which would not permit the Russian army to recover with the help of Lord Kitchener because the destruction of Czarist Russia had been determined upon. Lord Kitchener's death was caused by his abilities.'

10

The Riddle of the Empty Coffin

BY FAR the most active, persistent and prolific propagandist in demanding a new inquiry into the death of Kitchener and the loss of the *Hampshire* was Frank Power.

That, at least, was the name by which he was known to the *Sunday Referee* readers whom for some weeks he titillated with hints of the wickedness, treachery, gross incompetence and official skullduggery which, he alleged, surrounded the affair of the *Hampshire*. His real name was Arthur Vectis Freeman. He was not a sensational journalist either by profession or inclination. For many years he made a living as the editor of soberly respectable technical journals, as a correspondent of *The Times* and an author of serious tracts. He had always had a tremendous admiration for Kitchener; indeed, in the light of subsequent events, perhaps this admiration became something akin to an aberration. One of his earliest works was his *Letters from Khartoum*, written during the Siege of 1885. After his hero's death he was obsessed by a passionate desire to solve what he regarded almost as a 'national crime' and to probe the full story of the *Hampshire*'s loss.

In 1921 a film company known as the Seven Screen Plays produced a film entitled *How Kitchener Was Betrayed*, supposed to have been based on information supplied by Freeman. It dealt with the alleged betrayal of Kitchener through a woman and suggested that the Germans were aware, through the sinister influence of Rasputin, that Kitchener was sailing in the *Hampshire*. The film was shown privately to the sisters of the Field-Marshal and to certain members of the Lords and Commons.

As a result of this private showing the film was severely criticised on the grounds of its unsubstantiated allegation and bad taste. Pressure was brought to bear on the company either to scrap it or re-make it. This the company declined to do. Finally, the film was banned by the London County Council and, when an attempt was made to show it at the Leicester Square Cinema in November 1922, legal proceedings were instituted by the L.C.C.

Undeterred by the efforts of officialdom to thwart him, Arthur Freeman—or perhaps it is simpler to refer to him in future by his better known alias, Frank Power—undertook a nation-wide campaign by means of press articles and speeches to denounce the Admiralty for hiding the truth about the *Hampshire*. And on March 12, 1926, another film, entitled *The Tragedy of the 'Hampshire'*, was exhibited by United Films, Ltd., at the London Opera House. An announcement declared the occasion to be 'a great mass meeting' to support 'a national movement for the publication of the report of the Court of Inquiry'.

'The proceedings today,' said the *Manchester Guardian*, in reporting the event, 'were conducted by Mr. Frank Power, who began by asking his audience to stand for thirty seconds as a tribute to Kitchener. There had been a policy of hush-hush all along, he alleged. . . .

'The film was an interesting one in itself, but naturally had little bearing upon this series of accusations. Afterwards about half a dozen of the survivors of the *Hampshire* appeared on the platform and were cheered. At the end Mr. Power asked the audience to vote for a resolution demanding an inquiry.

'He said that it was passed unanimously, but a man in the meeting got up and said that the vote was not unanimous. By this time the meeting had been worked up to an emotional pitch, and there were loud cries of "Traitor" and "Throw him out".

'The audience no doubt contained some film experts interested in the technical side of the enterprise, but it seemed to be chiefly composed of people who are sympathetic to the idea that there is some undivulged mystery in the story of Kitchener's death.'

Almost as an aside, the *Guardian* added that this emotional audience included 'the representatives of some of the dominions and several members of Parliament.'

Some 2,000 people signed Power's petition for the publication of the full report on the disaster. And, no doubt encouraged by the response of a credulous public, Power made a sensational revelation in the press that Kitchener's body had been washed ashore in Norway and buried there. He announced his intention of going to Norway to bring back the body and inviting the co-operation of the Government and the Field-Marshal's relatives.

For some reason or other officialdom was coy about responding to Power's invitation. While they may well have been very dubious about his fantastic allegation and felt it could be safely ignored, they certainly made no effort to thwart him. Nor did they take any steps to refute his story. Mr. A. C. Fox-Davies, the former member of the Naval Law Branch of the Admiralty, commented in an article in the *Daily Express* on April 7, 1926, that he had heard that 'the body of a British officer was washed ashore and is now buried in a tiny Norwegian cemetery as that of an unknown.' And, he added, 'there are reasons for thinking that it may have been the body of Kitchener.'

If Mr. Fox-Davies, with his personal knowledge of the investigations, could make this comment, could it be that Admiralty experts thought likewise at this time?

Eventually a coffin in a large wooden packing case arrived at Southampton. It was said to have come from Norway to Newcastle by one ship and from Newcastle to Southampton by another. This seemed odd in itself, especially as the names of the vessels were not disclosed by Power, who personally received the coffin at Southampton. He declared that he identified the packing case by a knot in the wood as the one he saw in Norway ready for shipping. The coffin, he said, was one made especially for Lord Kitchener ten years previously and sent to Orkney in case the Field-Marshal's body should be found.

Power received a receipt—S-12 92271—from the Southern Railway for one coffin weighing 407 lb. The weight is an important factor in this story: it suggests that the coffin contained at least the equivalent weight of a body.

Power told the press: 'I am going to get in touch with the Government. I intend to hand over the coffin to the Prime Minister or his secretary, leaving them to take whatever steps they think necessary.

'The body is enclosed in three coffins, one within the other. The first is an elm casket, the second one of elm and copper and the third of polished elm. There is no inscription.'

The packing case was brought to London and on August 16, 1926, it was opened at the Lambeth mortuary in the presence of the Westminster Coroner, Mr. Ingleby Oddie, and Sir Bernard Spilsbury, the pathologist. The greatest secrecy was observed and before any official announcement was made, a long conference was held at the Home Office, attended by Chief Inspector Wensley. Frank Power was not present at the opening of the coffin or at the inquiry which followed.

Then came this laconic statement from the Home Office: 'The case in which it was alleged were the remains of Lord Kitchener was opened today. It was found to contain an apparently newly made coffin, but no human remains. The coffin had apparently never contained any human remains.'

Consultations between Home Office officials and Scotland Yard followed and Frank Power had a long interview with police chiefs at the Yard. Afterwards Power laughingly told a *Daily Mail* reporter:

'I have the Home Office in a quandary. They can bring no charge against me; I have not made any false declaration.

'The shell of the coffin is not the one which was originally placed there. I placed a private mark on it and it was absent when I examined the shell which was in the outer coffin and copper casket now in the possession of the police. I distrust officialdom intensely and I was frankly disappointed that I was not allowed to be present when the coffin was opened. I did not demand to be present, but I was assured that my presence was not necessary. However, I went to the mortuary in time to be present at the opening of the coffin, but was refused admission.

'I purchased the coffin with its copper casket and inner shell at Kirkwall in Orkney. It had lain for ten years in a mortuary at Lyness.'

Mr. T. Hurry, a Waterloo Road undertaker, was present at the opening of the coffin. 'Before I even touched it,' he told the *Evening Standard*, 'I knew that there was no body there. The lid of the coffin was not even fastened down, and it was evident that no undertaker had been employed on it. I initialled the packing case and I had to answer questions concerning my absolute certainty that what was opened was the identical packing case and coffin which Mr. Frank Power had asked me to take to my private mortuary.'

Mr. Hurry had been telephoned by a man who gave his name as 'Fraser', and asked to go to Waterloo Station and collect a packing case. He was told that the packing case contained a body and asked to 'treat it reverently'.

When Mr. Hurry arrived at the station an official asked him whether there was a corpse in the packing case. Mr. Hurry, who had not then handled the case or examined it, said he understood there was, whereupon he was asked to pay an extra £4 for the carrying of a corpse which apparently had not been declared when the packing case was put on the train at Southampton.

The police discovered an almost indecipherable word on

the packing case and decided that it was 'Kirkwall'. But inquiries in Orkney showed there was no trace there of any coffin having arrived from Norway addressed either to Power or Fraser. As there was no direct communication between Orkney and Norway any such case would have to be transhipped at Leith. There were only four possible means of entry into Orkney —by one of the two shipping companies trading to Kirkwall, by the steamer trading to Stromness, and by the mail steamer which crossed daily from Scrabster. Representatives of each of the transport companies stated that no such case, nor any case which might answer to the description, had come to the islands recently.

But a Mr. Backie confirmed that Frank Power had bought what had become known as the 'Kitchener coffin' on a visit to Orkney in connection with the unveiling of the Kitchener Memorial on Marwick Head.

The inquiries continued. It was learned that three weeks previously a coffin was shipped *from* Kirkwall to Newcastle, addressed to Frank Power. This case was included in the cargo of the steamer *St. Magnus*, which sailed from Kirkwall on July 27. But on the arrival of this vessel at Leith the following day, its contents were dispatched to Newcastle by rail.

A few days later support for the theory that the whole affair was a hoax came from the Norwegian newspaper *Stavangeren*, which gave details of a sham funeral of Lord Kitchener staged at Stavanger. 'A casket draped with the British flag was placed on a carriage drawn by two white horses and slowly conveyed to a Norwegian ship lying at Stavanger quay.

'Mr. Power apparently acted as priest, but there was some difficulty in developing the right shade of grief among the procession of mourners. A cinematograph camera clicked the whole time. Pictures were also taken of a grave and a real funeral was filmed at a local cemetery.

'The coffin was sent back to a carpenter's shop after the procession and Mr. Power paid those who followed as "mourners".'

Representatives of *Stavangeren* searched every churchyard and cemetery along a 50-mile stretch of coast around Stavanger and found not the slightest sign of a disturbed grave, or any evidence that a coffin or body had been removed. Clergymen who were interviewed all said that no one had sought permission to disinter any body.

* * * * *

The episode of the empty coffin was quickly forgotten as it became obvious that officialdom had been hoaxed. Although this may seem an irrelevant digression from the main theme of this book, it is important for various reasons. First, it illustrates the credulity of the public and Members of Parliament in accepting fantastic allegations by Frank Power and others. For months it aroused wide public interest, despite the fact that Power's reports had been dubbed 'ridiculous and wicked fabrications' by the First Lord of the Admiralty. Secondly, it is important to recall the case because it left an impression, largely confirmed by the publication of the Admiralty White Paper later the same month, that any mystery about the sinking of the *Hampshire* was finally disposed of and that that was the end of the matter. Most conveniently the incident of the empty coffin provided officialdom with an admirable opportunity to quash all further rumours at a moment when the public had at last become convinced that officialdom was fully vindicated and the rumours of years past entirely wrong.

While one must accept the evidence that the finding of Kitchener's body was a hoax, there were still many questions unsatisfactorily answered. Why, for example, did not the Government forestall Mr. Power by making their own inquiries as to whether Kitchener's body had been washed up in Norway? Why did not they call his bluff, or at least make inquiries through the consular services in Stavanger and elsewhere in Norway? If Kitchener's body had really been found and brought over in a packing case by a private individual in no way connected with the Field-Marshal's family, those in authority would certainly have looked remarkably silly. One can only imagine that they never believed Power would persist in his story to the extent of importing an empty coffin.

Why, too, was there such secrecy about the investigation at Lambeth mortuary, and why was Power not permitted to be present at the opening of the coffin? This merely provided Power with the alibi that there had been 'a substitution of one coffin for another'.

Then there was Mr. Fox-Davies' belief—referred to earlier in the chapter—that Kitchener's body might have been washed ashore in Norway and buried there. He had stated himself that 'I had through my hands every single paper the Admiralty possessed about the matter'. After the episode of the empty coffin the Admiralty White Paper found it necessary 'to contradict the rumour that has recently been given currency to the effect that bodies of officers and men belonging to the *Hampshire* were subsequently washed up on the Scandinavian coast, and that it is probable that Lord Kitchener's remains may have been buried there. The bodies recovered and buried on that coast after the sinking of the *Hampshire* were those of officers and men who lost their lives in the Battle of Jutland a few days previously. None of the *Hampshire*'s dead have ever been identified and buried on those shores and there are good reasons for regarding it as most improbable that the sea would have carried them there.'

Perhaps the biggest puzzle of all is why no action was taken by the authorities against Frank Power. Despite police inquiries and statements taken from him by the police no prosecution for creating a public mischief was brought. And the irony of the episode was that Power, far from helping to solve the mystery, only helped to destroy the idea that there was a mystery. After pestering the authorities for years to publish the facts, he ended up providing them with the perfect alibi for not doing so.

The appearance of the White Paper added little to what was already known, and some of its statements are palpably inaccurate. Security arrangements for the Russian mission were appallingly bad, and leakages occurred; yet the White Paper complacently says: 'The secret of Lord Kitchener's Mission was strictly guarded at the Admiralty where only five or six persons who were actually concerned with the arrangements knew what was in contemplation. The rumour that a request for secrecy was issued to the Press with so much detail that it defeated its own ends was dealt with by the Home Secretary in the House of Commons on the 29th June, 1916, when he denied emphatically that any communication whatever in regard to Lord Kitchener's Mission was issued to the Press before the loss of the *Hampshire*.'

The allegations made by Frank Power, Sir Richard Cooper, M.P. and others, that spies had been found aboard the *Hampshire* and shot, were fully refuted by the White Paper, and, in the absence of any further evidence, one must accept the Admiralty's explanation. In any case, even if spies had been found at Belfast and shot, it could not have had the slightest bearing on the events which followed. But as Sir Richard Cooper was so categorical in his letter to the *Daily Telegraph* ('The fact is that spies had been found in the *Hampshire* and had been shot'), the Admiralty's answer must be given.

'There is not the slightest ground for attributing to her (the *Hampshire*) a "bad record" in the matter of spies,' asserted the White Paper. 'A single spy scare which occurred whilst she was refitting at Belfast is apparently the foundation of all the rumours of this nature which have since been circulated, and it has, therefore, been thought worthy of investigation.

'The matter does not seem to have been reported to the Admiralty at the time—perhaps naturally enough, as it proved to be a mare's nest. The facts have, however, been established through the Military Officer who was in charge at Belfast Harbour and Shipyards at the time, and the then Senior Naval Officer, and are as follows.

'While the ship was refitting the captain of the *Hampshire* called on the Military Officer to help to investigate the discovery by a sentry of a shell for one of the small guns, which had been found on the main deck, with its fuze unscrewed, and covered by a piece of waste. The investigation elicited the fact that a shipyard worker who had been at the front as an artilleryman had noticed in a batch of shells, which was being moved for purposes of the refit, "a new kind of nose", and out of curiosity had taken one of the shells and unscrewed the fuze.

'Being disturbed in this act by a sentry, he had hidden the shell, which the sentry then found. The fact that precautions were taken and that a confidential investigation had been held was whispered about the ship, and the tale grew into the full-blown myth of an infernal machine in the magazine, an electric wire from the deck, and two spies in officers' uniform arrested and shot.'

The White Paper, however, did not satisfactorily dispose of criticisms of maladroit handling of the rescue arrangements, and the Admiralty's assertion that the Stromness lifeboat was not prevented from setting out must, in the light of independent evidence, be rejected.

Many questions previously raised were not mentioned at all. There was Sir Henry Dalziel's inquiry in the Commons about the mysterious vessel flying the Dutch flag which was seen immediately before the *Hampshire* reached the spot where she sank. The White Paper made no reference to this, yet Mr. Fox-Davies, having sifted all the evidence, declared: 'How six mines were laid is not known for certain, but there was afterwards a shrewd suspicion that a small fishing vessel flying the Dutch flag which had been seen several days before had something to do with it. She had been treated as a neutral and left alone. Whether she was really a Dutch or a German ship flying false colours, few will ever know.'

Now, even accepting the fact that the mines were laid by U75, as the White Paper claimed, the presence of this vessel at that time is surely a matter of some importance. It may be argued that as experts were convinced that the mines had not been laid by a surface vessel, the whole question was irrelevant. But Mr. Fox-Davies, who had been an 'active service' Naval officer before joining the legal branch of the Admiralty, believed it to have some significance. Why was this ship not traced? Why, indeed, was it left alone when, on the evidence of at least five civilians in the area, it had been cruising around for apparently no reason. An Orkney fisherman, Peddie, saw the supposed Dutch vessel and reported it. He was suspicious because it had 'an exceptionally powerful radio installation which was very rare in those days in any small fishing vessel.' After the war, when he heard reports of the sabotage of the *Hampshire*, Peddie went to the Admiralty to offer evidence. He declared that he was given short shrift and that 'they declined to take any statement from me'.

11

The Tell-tale Signal

THE ideal decipherer is often one who is not a native of the country for whom he is working. This is axiomatic in espionage, but it is a point not always appreciated by naval and military staffs.

In the Marine Section of Colonel Nicolai's listening post at Neumunster in the spring of 1916 a Norwegian named Lange was employed in the small deciphering staff. He was considered reliable and painstaking and had originally been recruited because of his experience as a wireless operator aboard merchant ships and, more important still, because of his detailed knowledge of British shipping routes.

Lange had started work for his German masters as a wireless operator, but he had quickly shown that he was not only able to take down messages, but to decipher them as well. Such versatility was unusual, if not unprecedented and at first Lange's superiors were chary of transferring him to the cipher department. But as they were short of professional decipherers, especially those who understood naval terminology, they set aside their qualms and gave him a chance.

From that day Lange was an unqualified success, much to the disgust of the aged professors who regarded deciphering as work fit only for a man with a university degree.

It was on the evening of May 26, only a few days before the Battle of Jutland, that Lange made what later proved to be the most remarkable *coup* of his career. He was on edge that night, for although he did not know what the German Naval Command were planning, he sensed that something big was afoot. He was irritated not only because he could not discern what was being planned, but because he had not picked up a worthwhile message from British naval sources for some days.

The Germans, though they had no organisation to compare with that of Admiral Hall in his Room 40 at the N.I.D. headquarters, had nevertheless been fairly successful in deciphering wireless messages from British ships. One can doubt their claims that they always found the key, but they broke down codes and ciphers often enough to obtain accurate intelligence of what went on across the German Ocean.

Earphones on his head, hands almost lazily turning the switches of his receiving set, the operator in the room above the cipher department yawned deeply and glanced at the clock. Another ten minutes to go and he would be able to leave his set and enjoy a glass of lager at a nearby mess.

Suddenly he jerked upright, adjusted the phasing and oscillator controls on the panel before him, reached for a pad and started jotting down symbols. Then, almost in disgust, he threw down his pencil and yawned again.

In due course the page from his signal pad was passed down to Lange. He read it through, translated and puckered up his face in bewilderment.

'Odd,' he said aloud, as though to himself. 'Very odd that they should be so anxious to tell the Admiralty. Surely it's purely a local matter.'

'What is that?' asked his fellow decipherer. 'A message to the Admiralty? Something worthwhile at last, eh?'

'Look here, I think you had better read it yourself. See what you make of it.'

His German colleague scribbled away for a few moments. Then, dully, he added: 'I see nothing to make a fuss about. It's unimportant.'

'Exactly, Otto. It's because it is unimportant that it is so very *important*. Here is a message from a British destroyer to the Admiralty saying that a channel west of Orkney has been swept free of mines. That, as you say, is nothing to make a fuss about. All right. But it's very odd all the same. Why should they report this direct to the Admiralty and not to the shore station?'

'Perhaps they mixed up their call signs.'

'That is impossible in the Royal Navy. They do not make such mistakes.'

'Well, perhaps the Admiralty has asked for a special report from that area.'

'Yes, but why have they not asked the Commander-in-Chief? And why should a destroyer make this report? Perhaps she was passing on a message from a minesweeper, but she didn't say so.'

'And what do you say we should do about it? Ring up Colonel Nicolai?' inquired Otto sarcastically.

Otto was a little jealous of the Norwegian newcomer to the cipher department.

Lange made up his mind: 'I'm going to question the telegraphist. And I'm going to warn his relief to see whether this message is repeated.'

Otto laughed: 'You take life more seriously than the High Command,' he jeered.

A few minutes later Lange returned to the room in triumph. 'What did I tell you,' he exclaimed. 'That message has been repeated already. Repeated three times. I know it before I have translated.'

Sure enough, when translated, the three signals he had brought in, proved to be exact repetitions of the earlier message. Evidently the wireless operator of the British ship was so anxious for the message to be safely received by the Admiralty that he had transmitted it four times in one hour.

And now Otto was prepared to take notice. He hated being baffled, but he was even more anxious not to let the Norwegian get all the credit. He went through each message carefully to see whether there were any variations. There was one: at the end of the last message was a word he could not translate. It was probably not meant to be a word at all, but was a slip-up in transmission. But Otto was convinced it meant 'urgent'.

There must be a great deal of urgency about this message, he argued, otherwise it would not have been repeated three times. But if somebody wanted the Admiralty to know that this area had been swept free of mines it could only be because the information was of vital importance to London. Why could that be? He suspected that the answer was that an important ship was to take this route and that the Admiralty had to be advised that it was clear of mines.

Lange, however, disagreed with him. He argued that he knew all these sea routes round Orkney and the north coast of Scotland intimately, and that there was no route for major shipping in this area.

'It is nonsense to say any important transport would go that way. There must be another explanation.'

But Otto, who had no knowledge of naval matters, insisted that his interpretation was right. And, in view of what transpired, on this occasion the non-expert proved right and the expert wrong.

Otto decided to use his own initiative. He telephoned through to Colonel Nicolai's offices and reported the message. At first he was sternly reprimanded and told that it was not his business to decide what should be a priority message. That was a task for the duty intelligence officer.

'But, sir,' said Otto. 'The circumstances are so unusual that I felt it my duty to let you know.'

The man at the other end of the line rang off abruptly. But just as Otto had told Lange it was all nonsense, and just as Colonel Nicolai's aide had rebuked Otto, so the aide, also seeking credit for himself, rang up the duty intelligence officer and asked him what he had to report.

Now it was the turn of the duty intelligence officer to be

rebuked. He had put aside the four messages in a pile marked 'non-urgent'.

Colonel Nicolai's aide took matters into his own hands. He telephoned Naval Headquarters in Neumunster. They, too, had picked up the message, but had not realised its significance.

'We had planned a very extensive series of minefields to be laid during the next few days,' said the German Admiralty spokesman. 'But the exact area mentioned in this message had not been regarded as important. Only a few minor coastal vessels use that route. However, it is as well not to leave any loophole. Perhaps the British Admiralty has decided that because this route has not yet been used by warships, that is a very good reason why they should use it in future.'

So the High Command's plan to seal off the northern approaches to Britain with a series of minefields was speedily amended. News of Lord Kitchener's impending mission to Russia had reached Naval Intelligence, but, as they had had no intimation what route he was likely to take, no special steps had been taken. In the light of the message intercepted that night it seemed possible that this might be the very route he would take.

Mine-laying submarines had been warned to stand by; it was felt that the use of surface craft might lead to detection of the German plan, which was to seal up the British Naval ports before the German Fleet put to sea. The U67 was detailed to lay mines off the Dogger Bank, UB21 and UB22 to close the approaches to the Humber, U67 to operate off the Tyne, U47 off Kinnaird Head and U44 off Scapa Flow, while U32, U51, U52 and U63 were to lay mines at strategic points in the North Sea. This was the master-plan to lure the British Grand Fleet to destruction.

At the last moment instructions went out to the submarine mine-layer U75, commanded by Ober-Leutnant Kurt Beitzen, to proceed at full speed to the west coast of Orkney and lay mines on the specified route.

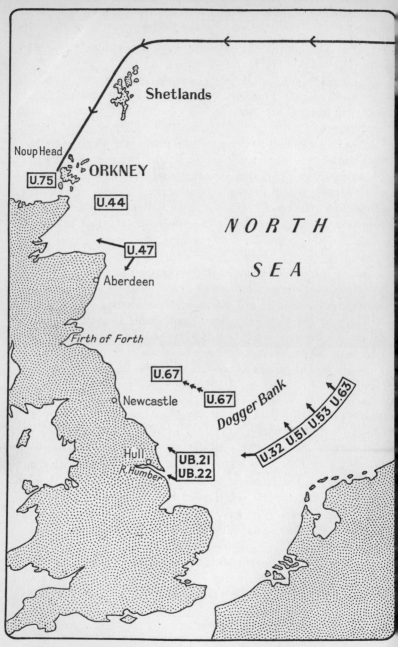

Position of German submarines towards the end of May, 1916

This was the first time that mine-laying submarines of a new type had been dispatched to British Fleet bases. In the report, dated July 4, 1916, of Admiral Scheer, Commander-in-Chief of the German High Sea Fleet, on the Battle of Jutland, these operations are referred to:

'In the middle of May I dispatched all submarines to sweep through the northern portion of the North Sea and to take up positions off the enemy's main bases—i.e. Humber, Firth of Forth, Moray Firth and Scapa Flow, from 23 May onwards, and then to compel the enemy to put to sea, by making an advance with our Fleet, and to give battle under conditions favourable to us. . . . German Plan II shows the areas to be swept by the submarines and their distribution off the enemy's harbours.'

This plan, to which Admiral Scheer referred, indicated the dispositions already mentioned and also shows the track of U75 to and from the waters west of Orkney. It will be noted that U75 set out for her destination on May 28, five days after the other submarines, which would seem to confirm that she was given a special mission.

U75 was already at sea when these late instructions were given to her. She was somewhere off the north coast of Norway, and the German Official History of the War by Sea (*Der Krieg zur See*, *Nordsee Band V*) describes U75's passage from the Norwegian coast to the north of the Shetlands and then on to Orkney.

Conditions were far from good; an overcast sky and fog made observations impossible and accurate navigation difficult. 'It then cleared up,' states the German report, 'and about 1.10 a.m. Noup Head Light was sighted. It had been ascertained that a route used by warships ran about two miles from the coast to the south of this point—i.e. from Noup Head, on the N.W. Coast of Westray, Orkney, to a position between Marwick Head and the Brough of Birsay, and U75 was to mine it. This was done. Between 6.0 and 8.35 a.m. the cargo of 22 mines was laid in several detached groups, about 7 metres below high water, after which she returned home; there was no interference whatever from the enemy's patrols.'

*   *   *   *   *

Kurt Beitzen failed to return from an operation in his last U boat, U102, on September 3, 1918. It is believed that U102 was sunk off the west coast of Ireland. He had left U75 before that boat was destroyed.

On May 4, 1917, the British steamer *Palmbranch*, laden with munitions, poison gas and high explosive, was zig-zagging her way towards the entrance of Kola Inlet on the Murman coast. Suddenly one of the guns' crews saw a stationary periscope sixty yards distant on the port beam. At the same time a white track of bubbles, indicating a torpedo's course, raced towards the ship. The track passed only a few yards from her stern, but the torpedo was too deep to strike her. The gun's crew of an American 13-pounder slammed to the breech and laid their sights to zero. As they did so the conning tower of a submarine rose on the port quarter; then the deck itself emerged.

The naval gunners had the submarine at point blank range. With alacrity they accepted this rare stroke of good fortune and their gun blasted the base of the conning tower. But danger was not averted. Though this submarine was sunk, another swiftly appeared three miles distant and opened fire. Luckily for the *Palmbranch*, the shells from the submarine's 4-inch guns missed their target, otherwise, crammed as she was with high explosive, she would have been blown out of the water.

It seemed odds on the U-boat winning, for she was a smaller target, had greater speed and a much heavier armament. Then, just as the *Palmbranch*'s captain was preparing to burn his charts and secret papers, a shell from the British ship knocked out the after-gun of the submarine. It was the turning point in the action; the U-boat abandoned her attack and headed for the open sea.

The crew of the *Palmbranch* reported that when the first submarine was sunk, a conical object floated from her and remained on the surface. This was a telephone buoy such as was used by U-boats to enable a sunken crew to communicate with the world above. Four weeks later a buoy answering this description was found by some Lapp fishermen at Dvorovaya Bay: it bore a large brass plate on which was inscribed '*Nicht offnen. Telefonbote liegen lassen! Telegraphieren sofort Liegestella an U Bootswen, Kiel. Unterseeboot 75 hier gesunken.*' (Do not open. Leave telephone buoy lying! Telegraph immediately position to U boats base, Kiel. Submarine 75 sunk here.)

Thus were the deaths of Kitchener and the officers and men of H.M.S. *Hampshire* avenged by a British merchantman.

German and British sources are at variance as to whether U75 was dispatched to lay mines west of Orkney because of information received that the Kitchener mission was due to leave for Russia, or solely on the strength of the message intercepted by the Neumunster listening station.

The account of the Neumunster incident, as described at the beginning of this chapter, was given to me by Herr Otto Kruger, a German who, during World War II, volunteered his services to the British intelligence in North Africa and subsequently became an import-export merchant in Tangier. Herr Kruger claimed to be the man who telephoned the destroyer signal through to Colonel Nicolai's office.

There are other substantiated versions of this story of events at Neumunster. In 1934 the *Berliner Illustrierte Zeitung* claimed that a decoder at the wireless station at Neumunster, whose job it was to decode enemy messages, drew the attention of the German High Command to a report to the British Admiralty from a destroyer that, according to instructions, a certain channel west of Orkney had been searched and found free of mines. The decoder 'assumed that the message was of special significance because it was transmitted three times in one hour. As a result orders were given for mines to be laid on this route.'

The Berlin correspondent of the *Morning Post*, in re-telling this story, referred to its author, 'whose strict anonymity, yet apparently free access to official sources, suggests that he may be an ex-naval officer, perhaps still employed in the Marine Section of the Ministry of Defence.' But it is by no means sure that this surmise was correct. There is no reference to this deciphered message in any official papers of the German Admiralty that have been published, and, according to Otto Kruger it is extremely unlikely that details would have been circulated outside Colonel Nicolai's department.

The writer of the article in the *Berliner Illustrierte Zeitung* claimed that U75 laid thirty-four mines, whereas the German *Official History of the War by Sea* said that twenty-two mines were laid, while the British Admiralty mentioned thirteen mines having been swept later in the month of June in the position mentioned. Mr. Fox-Davies stated that 'the Germans usually laid mines in chained sixes, and four were swept up after the storm abated.'

So there is no certainty about how many mines were actually laid off Marwick Head by U75. German naval experts with whom I have spoken do not think that Kurt Beitzen could have been carrying a full cargo of mines when he received the final signal from the German Admiralty. They regard twenty-two as the 'absolute maximum' of mines that he could have been carrying. The Admiralty White Paper does not make the position any clearer: it merely says 'the matter was settled beyond reasonable doubt by the discovery on 8th June of a group of moored German mines near the position where the *Hampshire* had last been seen.'

If three or more groups of mines had been laid in the vicinity, it might seem strange that there were not more casualties during the night of June 5 and the early morning of the following day, when destroyers and other craft were in the area.

There may be a rational explanation why the mines did no other damage on this occasion. In the deep water in which the U75 was directed to lay her mines at a depth of seven metres below high water, the tidal current would necessarily cause them to 'dip' and to lie deeper, except at slack water. Small merchant ships could have passed over these mines at all times unharmed. Indeed, even the *Hampshire* herself could, at most times of the day or night and in most weather, have sailed over them quite safely. It was only possible for the cruiser to hit one at dead low water, or when the ship was pitching heavily in a strong head wind. And the most ironic aspect of the tragedy was that these conditions were only fulfilled at the time the cruiser passed by Marwick Head.

The British Admiralty's view was that the mines were not laid where they were intended to be. There are some reasons to support this theory, but they are not conclusive. True, the German report admitted that 'frequent encounters with fog and an overcast sky had made observations difficult'. But the Germans claimed that the mines were laid in the right place on 'a route used by warships about two miles from the coast between Marwick Head and the Brough of Birsay'.

This may be so, but the Germans were wrong in thinking this was a normal warship route. Either their intelligence was faulty—in that small merchantmen were mistaken for warships —which seems unlikely, or they assumed from the signal from the British destroyer that, if this area had been swept, warships were intended to use this route. The latter explanation certainly fits the facts.

Even so, there is no doubt that the normal swept channel for auxiliaries and merchantmen was a little to the west of where the cruiser was mined. '

A footnote to the White Paper says: 'It is not easy to explain why mines obviously intended to destroy capital ships should have been laid in such an unpromising position. If, however, it is permissible to suppose that U75 laid them under conditions that led her to mistake her position, and thought she was laying them in the entrance to Hoy Sound, her action would be explicable and would be in conformity with Admiral Scheer's account of the operations.'

In adding this footnote, the Admiralty overstates its case and tries to simplify an incident which is far from simple. It is unthinkable that Kurt Beitzen, a highly competent and experienced submarine commander, would mistake a position which he could easily fix in daylight for the entrance to Hoy Sound. Nor do any German reports suggest he was told to go there.

By June 5, when the *Hampshire* was sunk, U75 was safely back in German waters.

* * * * *

There are many puzzling features connected with the minelaying in these waters apart from those already mentioned. Three posers are particularly worth examining.

First is the mystery of the small Dutch fishing vessel flying the Dutch flag, mentioned by Mr. Fox-Davies, corroborated by Orcadian fishermen, but not referred to in the Admiralty White Paper. Otto Kruger was especially interested in this revelation, which he only heard of from me in 1946. He believed that it was almost certainly a German 'spy ship'; there were, he said, a number of such craft operating around the north of Scotland.

'If one could trace this ship, the answer to many riddles might be possible. It could even be that U75 laid some of the mines but that the mine or mines which sank the *Hampshire* were laid by this craft,' he said.

Maybe, but it seems unlikely. Kruger was quite emphatic that U75 was the only craft ordered to lay mines anywhere near this position; if the 'Dutch' vessel had done any mine-laying, then it was done unofficially.

Second is the case of the minesweeping drifter, *Laurel Crown*, raised in Parliament, but never satisfactorily answered. Admiral Groos, the German naval war historian, asserted that 'the British Admiralty and Naval Intelligence Department were so confused and distracted by the German victory over the British Navy at Skaggerak (Jutland) that they completely failed to notice (or, if they noticed, to act upon it) the sinking of a drifter, *Laurel Crown*, in the area where the *Hampshire* was to sail a few days later. Instead of altering the course of the

Hampshire because of this, they allowed the cruiser to sail straight into the minefield laid by U75 on May 29.

'The drifter sank on June 2. That the *Hampshire* should have taken this very route three days later was proof of the shattering effect of the Battle of Jutland on the morale of the British Naval intelligence.'

But to this statement the White Paper has an answer. 'A mine-sweeping drifter, *Laurel Crown*, passing through this area, was blown up by·exploding one of the mines which had been dragged by the sweeps into shallower water without being subsequently sighted,' states the report.

'The date of this occurrence was the 22nd June, but in a return of Losses of Ships subsequently published by the Admiralty, by a printer's error the date was given as 2nd June, which would have been three days before the loss of the *Hampshire*.

'This error led to a suggestion in the German *Official History of the War by Sea*, which has been repeated in the newspaper press, that the existence of a known minefield was negligently overlooked when fixing the route of the *Hampshire*. The correct date, viz. the 22nd June, as to which there can be no possible doubt, shows this charge to be absolutely unfounded.'

This is an answer, but Admiral Groos, who is still alive, insists that the drifter was sunk on June 2, and he refutes entirely the Admiralty's explanation.

An Orcadian, who declines to give his name, claims that the area 'in the immediate vicinity of the disaster had never been swept for mines until after the sinking of the cruiser. The mines which were then swept were covered with a heavy growth of seaweed, which proved that they had been there for many months.'

This same informant cannot recall the exact date on which the *Laurel Crown* was sunk, but he is quite definite that it was *after* the *Hampshire* had been hit. 'I was living in Stromness at the time and I am positive the date was between June 6 and the end of the month.'

Other Orcadians testify similarly, so it would seem that the German claim was, in fact, based on a printer's error.

The third puzzle is the identity of a German submarine commander named Amberger. I first came across this name in Admiral Sir William James' biographical study of Admiral Sir Reginald Hall, *The Eyes of the Navy*, in which he wrote: 'Amberger, who laid the mines that sank the ship in which Kitchener was going to Russia, mistook Marwick Head for Hoo, and laid them in the wrong position.'

At first sight this seemed to be a contradiction of the generally accepted assumption that Kurt Beitzen laid the mines. I wrote to Admiral James for a solution of this problem. He was, however, unable to remember for certain whether he obtained the name 'Amberger' from notes among Admiral Hall's papers, or from Admiral Sir Lionel Preston, then in command of Fleet Minesweepers. Admiral James assumed that Amberger was captured later on and that possibly he may have given a wrong name when interrogated by the British. There would have been no official records kept of these interrogations.

Admiral Sir Lionel Preston has some interesting comments to make on the identity of Amberger and on the affair of the *Hampshire* in general, though some of the points he has to make are at variance with German claims. For example, German sources insist that Kurt Beitzen was an experienced submarine commander often used for special missions. This is refuted, according to Admiral Preston, by British intelligence reports.

'When I became Director of Minesweeping at the Admiralty, I was permitted to follow all movements of mine-laying submarines in the Very Secret Room, where they were plotted,' writes Admiral Preston.

'I thus got to know each German submarine commander by his name and the ship he commanded. How far these names were absolutely accurate I cannot say, but Amberger was allotted to U80 and his area of operations was in the Minches.

'I understand, however, at a later date that a young submarine commander, whose first trip it was, as a commanding officer, was for some reason or other allotted the job of dropping his mines off the Hoo, and that there is no doubt whoever laid them, they were erroneously dropped off Marwick Head. This was Ober-Leutnant Kurt Beitzen and not Amberger.

'I can say this, the mysterious Amberger was never captured under this name, nor could he have had any part in the laying of mines off Marwick.'

The tracing of Ober-Leutnant Amberger was a difficult task. In Britain nobody could recall what happened to him, but there was a vague feeling that this submarine commander was regarded as 'somewhat of a mystery' by minesweeping officers. Admiral Groos could not recall his name. When I pressed him to check in the German War History index to see whether the name was listed, he agreed to make a search, but replied that no such name could be found in the archives.

At last a check in the lists of German submarine commanders showed that between 1915 and 1918 the U80 had three commanding officers—Korvetten-Kapitan von Glasenapp, Korvetten-Kapitan Gustav Amberger and Korvetten-Kapitan Scherp. Glasenapp and Scherp are both dead. Herr Max Scherp, a distant relative, confirmed that Korvetten-Kapitan Scherp was the last commander of U80 and said that this submarine was used 'primarily for secret missions and very special mine-laying assignments'.

But when I tracked down Korvetten-Kapitan Amberger, who is now nearly 72, to his home in Birkenstein, he could not help very much. 'I am so sorry but I am not in a position to provide the answers to your questions because I was not in command of U80 until August, 1917.'

One of the pieces of 'evidence' upon which the rumour-mongers based their claim that the Germans knew the route the *Hampshire* was to take was the report that some of the mines recovered off Marwick Head bore the inscription 'Death to Kitchener'.

This 'evidence' is a complete distortion of the facts. About a month after the cruiser sank Admiral Preston, with the assistance of a petty officer, personally dismantled a mine found ashore near Cape Wrath. This mine, on which were inscribed the words *Kurfels Kitchener*, was believed by Admiral Preston to have been laid by Amberger in U80.

A number of World War I German naval officers have been questioned about this incident. They all say that it was normal practice to mark torpedoes, bombs and mines with 'messages' to the enemy, and their view is that *Kurfels* was probably a mis-spelling of the word *Teufels*, meaning 'Devils', which was quite often used in conjunction with the name of a British or other Allied war leader at that time.

Admiral Preston says he has never discovered what *Kurfels* meant and that it was suggested at the time that it was a very rude word of lower deck vernacular. But the Germans translate the message as 'Let this mine send Kitchener to the Devil' and insist that it has no ruder meaning.

The question of tense is important here, and there is no means of checking whether it was intended to be future, present or past from the way the 'message' is phrased. It could equally mean 'Kitchener has gone to the Devil', which would be a sardonic reminder of German striking power. But all the Germans to whom I have spoken—and in each case the individual has been a naval officer (some ex-submarine commanders)—are emphatic that such 'messages' were always composed in the future tense.

'This was part of the psychological warfare,' one of them told me. 'It would be pointless to put such a message in the past.'

'But why,' I asked, 'should the name of Kitchener be put on a mine? As far as you were concerned, Kitchener, as War Minister, would be most unlikely to be in a ship off anywhere in the north of Scotland.'

'Surely,' was the reply, 'this is proof that we knew of the Kitchener Mission to Russia and wanted to frighten the British.'

I find this argument quite untenable, if one accepts the statement that this batch of mines was laid after the *Hampshire* disaster. Even if it were otherwise, the Germans would be unlikely to advertise their prior knowledge of the mission. It seems likelier that the inscription was put on the mine shortly after it was known that Kitchener was dead, and the object may have been to panic the British into believing that this may have been one of several mines laid purposely to destroy the War Minister.

To the British Minesweeping Department Amberger was well known and looked upon as rather a joke. Apparently his mine-laying exploits were marked by a series of blunders. 'He never seemed able to get to the right place,' says Admiral Preston, 'and although the Minches do not cover much water, merchant ships seldom suffered from his attentions. We looked upon Amberger as a dud.'

But was Amberger a 'dud' with a purpose? Indeed, in view of Amberger's categorical statement that he was not in command of U80 until August 1917, were the British intelligence mistaking Amberger for Glasenapp, or somebody else? Who, in fact, was fooling who? Was some mystery commander of a U-boat merely aiming to give the impression of being a 'dud' to mislead our naval intelligence?

Herr Otto Stoermer lends some credence to this theory. He is quite positive that some German mines were deliberately laid outside the normal swept channels to make the N.I.D. think the enemy were acting upon wrong information. 'You must remember that in 1914–18, while you were short of mines (and many of those you had were more dangerous to you than to us), we had plenty. We could afford to use mines for purposes other than destruction. And in our view it was often more important to fool the much vaunted N.I.D. than to sink ships.

'During 1916 and 1917 we used an ex-submarine commander for certain secret work in the area from the Minches, round Cape Wrath and covering Orkney and Shetland. His mission was to mislead British naval intelligence and to keep us informed about movements.

'One of his main aims was to maintain liaison with Irish Nationalists and to encourage them to carry out acts of sabotage against the British. He did not always go to sea in a U-boat, but more often in a surface craft wearing the Dutch flag.'

This could be the answer to the mystery of the Dutch vessel seen off Marwick Head shortly before the *Hampshire* went down.

Apart from German sources, there is only one other version of the interception of the tell-tale signal from a British ship. The French newspaper *Temps* in 1934 reported that Kitchener had 'fallen victim to the British intelligence service'. According to this paper, 'in one of the last nights of May' the British intelligence issued a report which mentioned Orkney. This message was repeated three times within an hour and was picked up by the Germans. It stated that British torpedo boats had reported that waters west of Orkney were free from mines. The Germans, assuming that something important was pending, gave orders for a U-boat to lay new mines on the spot.

This report does not tally exactly with that in the *Berliner Illustrierte Zeitung*. Otto Kruger thought that the story in *Temps* was a garbled version of what had already appeared in the German paper. 'The message we picked up did not come from the N.I.D. It came direct from a destroyer and it is, of course, nonsense that torpedo boats would have made such a report.'

Kruger, however, admitted that his department could not establish the identity of the destroyer sending the message, but he was quite certain that it was a destroyer's call sign. It may, therefore, be possible that *Temps* was not far wide of the mark. French informants were insistent that the message was repeated three times 'from a British intelligence source' and claimed that the signal was intended to mislead the Germans and cause them to lay mines in this area, where in normal circumstances they would have harmed nobody.

I quote from a statement by M. René Tarpin: 'I helped to compile a dossier for *Temps* on this affair, and our sources of information were both British and German. There is no doubt at all that there was an appalling blunder in the N.I.D., due to this department being so overwhelmed with work in connection with the Battle of Jutland. So great was their preoccupation with that battle that the message which they deliberately 'leaked' to the enemy was forgotten.

'So instead of misleading the Germans, they fell into the very trap they themselves had set. No one informed the Commander-in-Chief that mines might be laid in this area in consequence of the bait set for the Germans by the wireless message. The message was sent in a cipher which the N.I.D. knew the Germans had obtained; it was repeated three times so that they should not miss it. When the British Admiralty claimed afterwards that the mines were laid in the wrong place, they only told half the story. Naturally, for the truth would have been extremely embarrassing for them.

'This is the explanation for the original rumour that the British Secret Service engineered the death of Kitchener. It is as simple as that.'

The Germans, of course, would be unlikely to admit that what had seemed to them a *coup* for their deciphering experts was a trap set for them by the British intelligence.

M. Tarpin's version of events is feasible as far as it goes. Naval Intelligence had on a number of occasions used wireless to pass on false information on mine-laying and mine-clearance to the enemy. Admiral Hall himself had taken grave risks in carrying out such subterfuges without keeping Operations informed. Filson Young in his book *With the Battle Cruisers* told how 'in the little parish magazine of *Secret Intelligence*, that was served out to Commanding Officers afloat (the Admiralty) continued to report the *Audacious* as being with the Second Battle Squadron, although everyone in the Fleet knew she had been sunk in November, and the fact had been published in the American press.

'It was a good example of the somewhat childish point of view of Intelligence, in which it seemed to be held a clever thing to tell a lie, in the general hope that someone might be deceived. It was one of the more innocent of the ways in which we tried to imitate the Germans. When they told lies it was with a definite purpose: we told them without any purpose at all.'

This is perhaps a sweeping indictment, but it would indeed be ironic if the tell-tale message was one of the lies told 'without any purpose at all'.

Certainly it would seem that the Commander-in-Chief, Admiral Jellicoe, was not always kept fully informed of enemy mine-laying activities. His own statements reveal this, and it is hard to understand his optimism regarding the route he chose when it is borne in mind that an enemy submarine had been sighted west of Orkney at 9.15 on the morning of June 5. In this instance Jellicoe was informed shortly before noon by the Senior Officer of the Minesweepers. A patrol vessel claimed to have spotted the submarine north-east of Cape Wrath, but no further reports came in and no one could be sure that this piece of intelligence was correct. Jellicoe may have disregarded it. His liaison with various departments appears to have been inadequate, as is proved by the fact that the Minesweeping Department had not been consulted on the decision to use the western channel.

To sum up the story of the tell-tale signal, these seem to be the relevant points:

(1) The Germans say the mines laid by U75 were in the exact position given to the U-boat commander. Every document and source confirms this.

(2) The British Admiralty insisted that they were laid off Marwick by mistake. But they give no reasons for making this allegation. It is an unsubstantiated claim.

(3) Kruger and the *Berliner Illustrierte Zeitung* say the signal came from a British destroyer. In neither case was the identity of the destroyer indicated, and Kruger is emphatic that its

identity was never established. This may be a weakness in the German story, but it could well be that it supports the French statement about the signal coming from 'the British intelligence'. If the latter wished to put out a signal to fool the Germans, they would probably use the call sign of a fictitious warship, most likely a destroyer.

12

Saboteurs' Testimony

IMMEDIATELY after the sinking of the *Hampshire*, and again twenty years later, allegations were made that the cruiser had not been mined, nor torpedoed, but had been destroyed by an internal explosion, the work of enemy saboteurs.

When two Germans claim to have been personally responsible for killing Kitchener, and three writers publish books alleging that the Field Marshal's death was brought about by deliberate acts of sabotage, one cannot dismiss these allegations without at least examining them carefully, however strong the conflicting evidence appears.

The Admiralty White Paper is quite emphatic in rejecting any suggestion of sabotage. 'It is scarcely credible that any intelligent person can still venture to advance the hypothesis of an internal explosion caused by spies on board. Not a shred of evidence to support such an hypothesis has ever come to the knowledge of the Admiralty from any source whatever. On the other hand, it can definitely be stated that the destruction caused by a violent internal explosion would have been quite different in character from that which the *Hampshire* sustained, and that the evidence as to the effect of the explosion in the *Hampshire* is in itself strong proof that it was due to external causes.'

As in other instances in the White Paper, the authors overstate their case and lay themselves open to awkward questions.

The obvious question which this statement raises is what the 'evidence as to the effect of the explosion' was. The only possible evidence could have been obtained from the survivors, as, on the Admiralty's own admission, no inspection of the wreck was ever carried out by divers. This is not surprising when one considers that the cruiser was lying at a depth of forty fathoms in fast-running cross currents.

The problem of whether or not there had been an internal explosion could only be solved positively by a diver inspecting the plates of the vessel to see if the holes in her side had been torn outwardly from within, or inwards from without. A Naval officer who served at Scapa during World War I told me there was much discussion of the theory of sabotage at the time and that 'there was talk of a diver being sent down to settle the matter one way or another.'

It is worth noting that the major and most positive allegations of sabotage came not before the publication of the White Paper, but after it. This could well be because those making the claims were convinced that the Admiralty was not in a position to refute such allegations, having made no underwater inspection of the cruiser.

On June 23, 1934, the *Daily Telegraph* carried a report from its Ottawa correspondent which referred to 'the almost incredible statement that the loss of the British cruiser *Hampshire*, with Lord Kitchener aboard, was caused by two German Secret Service agents disguised as British sailors.'

The statement was made by Captain Borkowski of the Polish liner *Kosciuszko*, when his ship arrived at Halifax, Nova Scotia.

'Captain Borkowski, who served in the war with distinction, said that a few years ago when he was in Hamburg, the former commander of a German submarine told him that two Secret Service agents volunteered to destroy the *Hampshire*, knowing they would face certain death.

'Supplied with stolen passports, the two men reached Scotland, and, killing two members of the cruiser's crew, got on board in their places. Then, in some manner not explained, they reached and exploded the magazine.

'Captain Borkowski seemed reluctant to discuss the matter beyond giving a mere recital of the tale. He was not able to explain how it happened that two strangers coming aboard a Naval vessel could escape being immediately exposed by their shipmates. But he did not attach credit to the generally accepted belief that the ship was sunk by a floating mine.'

Three years previously sensational allegations had also been made in a book entitled *Die Weltkriegsspionage* by W. Bley. This was a lengthy diatribe against 'the evil machinations of the British Secret Service', and its general content was heavy, humourless, Teutonic melodrama. The author asserted, for example, that 'the British Secret Service was willing to sacrifice a fellow-countryman, even one with such a great record of service as Lord Kitchener, if, for policy reasons, it appeared necessary to do so.'

The policy of the British in World War I, argued the author, was 'not only the defeat of Germany, but the exhaustion of France and the permanent exclusion of Russia as a great power'. Therefore, the Secret Service opposed the plan to send Kitchener to Russia to advise in the re-organisation of the Russian armies, and they 'arranged' to have the *Hampshire* sunk in such a manner that it would not damage the Allied cause or Britain's reputation!

Most of Bley's narrative, like his theories of British policy, do not stand up to examination. He makes the fatuous suggestion that when the *Hampshire* was in Belfast for a refit in 1916 'the Head of the British Secret Service brought on board a number of boxes which were said to contain documents of such high value that it would be better for the ship to be blown up than for them to fall into enemy hands.'

While the cruiser was at Invergordon 'fourteen stokers deserted' because they were 'afraid of something mysterious aboard'. It was later reported that fourteen had been taken to the Tower of London and shot.

Needless to say there is no confirmation of any such claims. It is almost certain that the source of this dubious account was the material published by Frank Power.

Bley also stated that there were 'three explosions, clearly heard from the shore'. As we have already seen, the wind was so violent that the explosion, or explosions, could not be heard on the mainland. Then the author repeated an error perpetrated by Frank Power: 'the first lifeboat only took to sea five hours after the catastrophe, and it was recalled after covering three miles towards the *Hampshire*.' The lifeboat never put to sea.

As evidence that there was foreknowledge of the fate which awaited the cruiser, Bley said that 'five hours before the *Hampshire* sank an Irish Nationalist newspaper in Dublin published a headline "Kitchener Goes to Hell". A piece of this newspaper is in the possession of the Duke of Northumberland.'

There may be some grain of truth in this assertion, though doubtless it has been distorted. The late Frank Ryan, who was once Chief of Staff of the Irish Republican Army, told me he had seen a copy of the paper. So, too, did Admiral Sir Guy Gaunt, British naval attaché in Washington in World War I: he said that a copy of this underground broadsheet reached him in U.S.A. and that it contained a brief story about the assassination of Kitchener by a time-bomb placed in the ship that was carrying him to Russia. But neither the name of the ship, nor the site of the disaster were given; it merely mentioned somewhere off the coast of northern Scotland.

Admiral Gaunt said that he gave his copy of the paper to the Duke of Northumberland, who was particularly interested in Irish Nationalist affairs. The Duke served in the intelligence section of the War Office during the war.

The present Duke of Northumberland has no recollection of the 'piece of paper'. On the other hand, he says, 'it may well be so, as my father took a great interest in the cause of the Southern Irish Loyalists'.

One must remember that Bley's book was published between

the two world wars at a time when it was fashionable to besmirch Britain and to credit the most fantastic and monstrous deeds to the British Secret Service. Both in Germany and in France there was a belief that in some mysterious way the Secret Service was the originator of British foreign policy, and that successive governments accepted its rulings.

Dr. Erwin Weiss, some of whose views have already been mentioned, regards the opinions expressed in *Die Weltkriegsspionage* as 'far fetched'. But, he adds, 'there seems no doubt whatever that the explosion which caused the sinking of the *Hampshire* came from the interior of the ship, so that sabotage cannot be excluded, though in my opinion Kitchener's enemies in England and Ireland played their part in this.'

As Dr. Weiss is a specialist in German war history and has spent much time in making researches into the *Hampshire* disaster, he must be listened to with respect. He alone of the German war historians now living holds to this view.

'A sabotage act from the German side,' he said, 'I regard as out of the question, as the decision about the place and time of Kitchener's departure was only known to a few people a short time beforehand.

'The opinion of General Ludendorff that the sinking of the *Hampshire* was engineered from the Russian side I do not hold to be correct. Neither the old Czarist Officers' Corps, which certainly was not pleased with the suggestion that Kitchener should visit Russia, nor the revolutionary circles, which were interested in the defeat of the Russian Army, had at the time such extensive sabotage organisations as to be able to plan the sinking of such a vessel.'

The only other living German to support the sabotage theory is Dr. Paul Schmidt, Hitler's interpreter and former German Foreign Office official. He says that he always understood that the disaster to the *Hampshire* was due to the placing of an explosive charge in the ship's coal by German agents, aimed at creating the impression that the ship had hit a mine. Dr. Schmidt declines to elaborate on this statement, though he should be in a position to learn the truth from secret records.

In April 1932 a book by Clement Wood was published in New York, *The Man Who Killed Kitchener*. This book contained the most fantastic and detailed story of all about the fate of the *Hampshire*. It was the life story of a German spy, Fritz Joubert Duquesne, alias Captain Stoughton of the 'West Australian Light Horse', also known under the names of Frederick Fredericks and Piet Niacoud.

A brief summary of Duquesne's story will suffice to show how ridiculous it is. He was supposed to have started his spying activities on behalf of the Boers as a lad of seventeen. It was in this period that he developed a fanatical hatred of Kitchener, whom he swore to kill. While attending a banquet in honour of Kitchener at Cape Town, he was arrested by the inevitable 'British Secret Servicemen', was condemned to death, but secured his reprieve by offering to translate the Boer code. His sentence was then altered to imprisonment in 'an internment camp in the Bahamas'.

From these islands he escaped by jumping over a cliff and swimming through shark-infested seas. Then during World War I he offered his services to the Germans and was implicated in the sabotage of the British ship *Tennyson*. Arrested in the U.S.A., he feigned paralysis for seven months before once again making a dramatic escape.

The Man Who Killed Kitchener described how Duquesne posed as a Russian count, Zakrevski, who had been kidnapped by the Germans after they learned the secret of the Kitchener Mission to Russia from the count's pro-German fiancée. With the count's identity papers in his pocket, Duquesne reported to the British Ambassador in Copenhagen and was given authority to proceed to Britain. Apparently, having successfully posed as a Russian liaison officer, he had no difficulty at all in getting aboard the *Hampshire* as a member of Kitchener's party.

What happened once he was aboard the cruiser is enough to make a Hollywood scriptwriter envious. Duquesne immediately became the pin-up boy of every maiden in the German Reich. He used an 'electric torch' to signal for a German submarine to fire a torpedo at the ship, and, when the explosion occurred, he was 'standing by the bridge behind Lord Kitchener, ready to shoot him down, if there seemed the slightest chance of his escaping. In the next moment we were thrown into the water . . . Kitchener was never seen again.'

And Duquesne himself? Escape was simple enough, even in this raging storm. The man who had braved sharks off the Bahamas nonchalantly kept afloat on the mountainous waves, even managing to signal to the German submarine to rescue him. The U-boat raced towards him, the crew pulled him inboard and Fritz Duquesne, following the best traditions of the fairy story, returned to Germany in triumph to be created 'Baron of Brandenberg'.

For the record, Duquesne was without doubt a German agent. The *Daily Mail* of May 27, 1919, described him as 'the cleverest and most dangerous of the enemy agents', thus providing him just sufficient background for his preposterous claims. And he found, especially in U.S.A., that, by creating a myth about himself, he could achieve domination over lesser and more credulous agents. He was definitely implicated in the loss of the *Tennyson* off the coast of Brazil in February 1916, and on December 8, 1917, was arrested for fraud at Southampton.

After the publication of *The Man Who Killed Kitchener*, he was arrested in New York at the request of the British Government and the question of extradition proceedings was raised. When detained by the New York police Duquesne insisted that he was an Englishman named Frank Craven and that he had merely been a publicity agent for the book.

But somehow, either through his ability to bluff his way out of any situation, or his influence in high places, Duquesne was soon free again. And in the years before World War II he became once more, in the words of Attorney Harold Kennedy, 'the master-mind of the German spy ring in the United States'.

In 1941 he was arrested again in connection with a plot to blow up a big factory in Schenectady with a time-bomb.

No one, however, except a few credulous people in the U.S.A., seriously regarded Duquesne's claims to have killed Kitchener. His story is so obviously a work of fiction, at least as regards his version of the *Hampshire* disaster, that it can be dismissed without further examination.

The next claimant to have engineered the sinking of the *Hampshire* told a more plausible story. It is important to note the date of the publication of this narrative—1934. By this time one would have thought that any new version of the *Hampshire* episode on the lines of 'I killed Kitchener' would be almost impossible to publish in any country, and at the best treated with grave suspicion by any publisher. But Ernst Carl's *One Against England* was not only published by Reutlingen in Germany in 1934, but was immediately hailed by the official Government newspaper, *Volkischer Beobachter*, as 'an accurate account'.

Whatever may have been the first thoughts of *Volkischer Beobachter*, the second thoughts of the Nazi Government were to order the suppression of the book. On February 12, 1935, news came from Berlin that *One Against England* had been banned from all bookshops. In September of the same year an English translation of the book was published in Britain.*

According to Carl, he started industrial espionage before the First World War, stealing plans from the Goodrich Tyre Company. Certainly official records confirm his earlier exploits in espionage. *The Times* of November 5, 1917, stated that he was sentenced at Westminster Police Court for having stolen a kitbag from the Eccleston Hotel, where he was working as a porter. It was then stated by the police that the previous July he had been fined at Lambeth for failing to register as an alien.

Detective-Sergeant Purkiss said that Carl was regarded by the authorities as 'a spy and a dangerous man', who had served one year in the Bavarian Army and, on receipt of

One Against England: Jarrolds, 1935.

German military papers after the outbreak of war, had come to England. He afterwards stole a Swiss passport and posed as a Swiss. On one occasion he was found with £300 in his possession. He was sentenced to six months' imprisonment with hard labour, with a recommendation for expulsion.

In *One Against England* Carl claimed to have assumed the name of Jaggi from the identity and papers of a young Belgian officer killed in the German advance into Belgium in 1914. The documents and uniform of the Belgian were captured by the German espionage service, and it was in this uniform that he entered Britain in September, 1914.

He made contact with the Irish Republican movement, which the Germans were then actively supporting. His first meeting with Kitchener, he alleged, was when, again posing as a Belgian officer in uniform, he offered the War Minister valuable antiques which he said he had saved from the Germans. It was after this meeting that he personally conceived the idea of planning the assassination of Kitchener in collaboration with the Irish Republicans.

But Carl's version of what happened next is only valid if one accepts that the decision to send Kitchener to Russia in the *Hampshire* was known for several weeks beforehand. Otherwise it is impossible to see how such careful plans could have been laid. Any such assumption can, I feel sure, be ruled out entirely. Even if it were true, the dispatch of the *Hampshire* with the Grand Fleet to the Jutland action must certainly have led any conspirators to doubt whether they had received the right information.

Carl, however, insisted that he had obtained a list of the *Hampshire*'s crew under the pretext that he was a shipwrecked Dutch seaman named Vanoeven, and wanted to track down an old friend. This list was handed to the Irish Republican organisation so that they could check whether there was any Irishman aboard the cruiser who might be able to collaborate.

Eventually Carl established contact with two Irish members of the crew, found that they were violently pro-Nationalist and succeeded in inducing them to place time-bombs in the cruiser. The Irishmen were told 'Kitchener is the worst enemy of your Fatherland and your actions may result in Ireland's victory'. The sailors were promised that they would be enabled to escape to Ireland and given a reward in cash.

Carl then made the curious claim that threatening telegrams, which had been sent to the Admiralty in London, had the effect of getting the port of departure changed from Northern Ireland to Scotland. The implication of this can only be that, when the *Hampshire* was in Belfast for a refit, it had been decided to send Kitchener to Russia and that he was to have left from that port. But the refit was in February, when arrangements for the mission had not been made.

In due course Carl personally gave the time-bombs, 'packed in blankets', to the two Irishmen, who succeeded in stowing them away in the 'ammunition room' of the cruiser. Plans were then made for the Irishmen to flee to Ireland via the Hebrides.

Then came the dramatic finale. Carl went to a 'neighbouring S'—no name is given, just the initial—where he stayed at the 'White Horse Inn', and he and the Irishmen were thought to be sheep dealers from the Shetlands.

'We three stand in the window . . . the little dot below is the *Hampshire*. Our nerves are taut. We can see no movement of the ship. The clock finger moves slowly onward. We wait, wait, wait. It is two-thirty. Is the plot known and the ship's departure postponed? If it does not leave soon, the vessel will explode in the harbour. . . .

'Finally it leaves with the escort vessels. The *Hampshire* sails on a northerly course. Suddenly two columns of smoke rise one after the other from the ship. A few seconds later we hear the detonation. Our eyes are strained on the sinking vessel. Now the sea has swallowed her up.

'One of the Irishmen speaks: "Thus ends Lord Horatio Herbert Kitchener, England's marshal and Ireland's enemy. God protect Ireland!"'

How three people could manage to watch from the same

vantage point the departure of the cruiser and its subsequent sinking off Marwick Head is not explained. Nor can it be, if one takes even a perfunctory glance at the map. I have been unable to trace any inn with a name anything like the White Horse in Orkney. A scrutiny of a list of licensed premises then existing reveals no mention of it. It is practically certain that there was no inn from which the sinking of the *Hampshire* could be seen. Inns, as understood in England, are foreign to Orkney: an inn sign with a representation of a white horse, or anything like that, is never seen there. There is one hotel at Dounby, but that is well inland.

Later in his book Carl described a conversation which he alleged he had with a 'circle of officers and Parliamentarians. in the home of a 'well known English politician in London' some days after the *Hampshire*'s sinking. An official of the War Office is described as saying that 'the truth lies deeper. It is only valuable as far as it is useful. For official circles in Britain a mine or torpedo is regarded as the cause of the accident. Informed circles do not believe this. You, Maurice Hankey, and Lloyd George, had a premonition of the "mine" which you presume sank the *Hampshire* and you stayed at home.'

Carl also mentioned 'the SOS call which the *Hampshire* sent out a few minutes before she sank,' saying that it referred to 'an explosion inside the ship'. But no message of any kind was dispatched, as we have seen.

After the disaster he asserted that 'British official circles knew that Kitchener's mission had been betrayed in advance to the Germans and secret documents were no longer kept in London, but were hidden in the wine cellar of a British politician in Northumberland.' He also supported the claim that 'one Sinn Fein group is said to have announced the sinking of the Hampshire before she had done more than leave port'.

This last incident was also mentioned in Bley's book, and there are a number of interesting parallels between Carl's and Bley's versions of events, notably a reference to a 'number of boxes' which were put aboard the cruiser when she was refitting in Belfast. This story can be traced back to Frank Power and Sir Richard Cooper and is supposed to have originated from survivors of the cruiser who said there was 'something my-terious about the boxes'. Carl said he received news from Irish agents that 'big boxes had been taken aboard under heavy guard and that they came from the Bank of England'.

If any such boxes were taken aboard at Belfast, it is almost certain that they contained nothing more than ship's stores. It is quite ridiculous to suggest that bullion or anything else of value would be loaded during a refit.

Nevertheless, though many of his statements are not borne out by the facts, Carl's story is not dismissed quite so easily as that of Fritz Duquesne. It is of interest not because of its revelations, but because of the remarkable chain of coincidences which, indirectly, it brought to light. Investigation shows that it contains some grains of truth.

That Carl, or someone like him who masqueraded some-times as a Belgian and at others as a Swiss, had contacts with the Irish Republicans was confirmed by Frank Ryan, the I.R.A. leader who later fought for the Republicans in Spain. I had an interview with Ryan in Dublin in 1936 and we discussed the episode of the *Hampshire* in some detail.

Ryan hooted with laughter at the description of the Irish-man solemnly proclaiming Kitchener's death. 'I'm sorry if I sound irreverent,' he said, 'but no Irishman would talk like that. He would say "And that's the end of the poor ould English bastard."

'But, joking apart, there is some truth in this book by the German. There was an Irish plot to get rid of Kitchener and he had been watched by the Sinn Feiners for many weeks be-fore the *Hampshire* sank. The authorities suspected something was afoot and that was why they panicked when they heard the cruiser had gone down.

'But it is all nonsense to suggest this was a German plot organised by one man. I always understood there were two separate plots—one German and one Sinn Fein, but that after the arrest of Casement the Irish joined forces with the Germans.

'What came of this joint operation I don't know. I was too young to be in the know in those days. But I knew a Sinn Feiner who was in on the plot. He always said that Lloyd George let out the news about the Kitchener mission to Russia when he was in Ireland for the British Government about April, 1916.

'So that leakage may in some way have been confused afterwards with the fact that the *Hampshire* refitted in Belfast the previous February. Probably someone remembered the spy scare and then added one and one and made half a dozen.

'This Sinn Feiner was in Orkney at the time of the sinking. He returned to Ireland by fishing vessel via the Island of Lewis. He had to lie low for a long time as the English were looking for him. But he was sceptical about the success of any time-bomb plot. I gathered he was only in Orkney to report what happened. He heard there was to be an attempt to put a time-bomb in the cruiser and that it was scheduled to explode six hours after the ship left her anchorage.

'But he doubted very much whether anyone could have got aboard to place a time-bomb there. He was convinced the ship hit a mine and that possibly, but not probably, mark you, the explosion touched off the time-bomb, which accounted for the two explosions.'

In view of all this it seemed worth while trying to track down Ernst Carl. I learned that his book was suppressed by the German authorities because at that time—the Nazis were trying to curry favour in Britain—it was not politic to encourage anti-British books. At any rate Carl became a marked man and was involved in difficulties with the Gestapo. Perhaps he was suspect because he had an English wife; he had always maintained that the British never proceeded with espionage charges against him because of the intercession of his wife. Probably the Nazis thought it strange that he had escaped with so light a sentence and feared he might be spying against his own country.

He fled from Germany to Italy, stayed there for a year and went to the U.S.A. And after that there seemed to be a complete blank.

The firm which published his book in Germany no longer exists, but eventually I managed to find a former book-keeper of this firm who remembered that Carl had a brother who was living in Wuerttemberg. From the brother I learned that Carl was living in Brooklyn, U.S.A., under the name of Ernst Carl Gellrichsheimer, which apparently is his real name.

I wrote to Mr. Gellrichsheimer in the hope of obtaining the answers to several queries. The Americans helped him to escape from Italy when the Gestapo tracked him down there, and to-day, no doubt in gratitude, he is an American ctitzen. Immediately after the First World War he led an adventurous life in South America, Turkey and the Far East. During World War II he was sympathetic to the Allied cause: on this point there appears to be no doubt.

Since 1940 he has made a living as a journalist and his ambition is to retire to Madeira when he is sixty-five 'to keep up a villa in style at Funchal'.

'It is not in my interest, nor would the British Government like to see the Lord Kitchener story re-hashed,' he writes. 'In my opinion everything hasn't been told yet. Historians groped in the dark.

'*One Against England* was a story where truth and fiction are mixed. It was originally written for the Terra Films, Berlin, but the Nazis stopped it being filmed when Hitler took over.

'I was not a master, but only an apprentice during the First World War. I was the only survivor of my outfit, which made me "master" by inheritance.'

So, tantalisingly, one may still have to wait a long time for Carl's full story.

L.K.D.—M

13

The Strange Story of
Locksmith Courtney

IT is reasonable to ask at this stage why, in order to answer criticisms once and for all, the Admiralty did not send down a diver to examine the wreck of the *Hampshire*. By ascertaining whether the ship's plates were torn inwards or outwards, and by tabulating other evidence from the ship, the sabotage stories could quite easily be substantiated or finally refuted.

But before answering this query another remarkable story requires investigation—that of a secret attempt to salvage the *Hampshire*, carried out at the instigation of that enigmatic arms peddler, the late Sir Basil Zaharoff.

The first hint of the so-called salvage attempt was given in an Associated Press dispatch from New York on April 26, 1933. This mentioned very briefly that £15,000 in gold had been recovered from the wreck of the cruiser. Asked to comment on this information, the British Admiralty stated that they had 'no knowledge of any expedition to salvage the *Hampshire*'.

Then in December of the same year the *Berliner Illustrierte Zeitung* gave the story in much greater detail. Their informant was stated to be an American diver lying in a Berlin hospital, a Mr. Whitefield, variously described as 'a German deep sea diver' and 'of Norfolk, Virginia'. He claimed that a German vessel, flying the British flag, had been engaged on successful salvage work on the *Hampshire* and that, as a result, the crew had recovered from the wreck '£10,000 in gold bars, valuable personal papers relating to Lord Kitchener's mission and several British signal volumes'.

The salvage vessel was said to be docked in Konigsberg, undergoing a refit in preparation for a further salvage expedition. But when a *Sunday Chronicle* reporter made inquiries in the port, he 'failed to find evidence to substantiate this part of the story'.

Three expert divers, a German, an Australian and an American, were said to be in hospital after receiving serious injuries in a mud-slide that followed a perilous deep-sea explosion as they blasted their way into the cruiser's 'strong rooms'.

Salvage operations were said to have been begun two years previously. They were then unsuccessful, though the *Hampshire*'s position was definitely fixed. The vessel returned to Kiel and a new and successful attempt with the latest salvage equipment was made in April 1933.

The names of the three diving experts were given as: Costello, an Australian with a long experience of difficult salvage operations; Charles Courtney, a master locksmith, and Whitefield. It was never quite clear whether Whitefield was supposed to be American or German.

To avoid suspicion about his plans the captain of the salvage vessel, which was not named, took a roundabout route from Kiel, cruising along the Norwegian coast, then steaming back along the same course before heading for Orkney. For a week the divers worked in shifts, clearing away the sand and mud from a great hole in the wreck.

The report stated: 'After considerable discussion it was decided to plant three time-bombs over the wreck and to blow it up. This plan was carried out at great risk. The bombs were placed and exploded. But when the divers again descended to the wreck a second and unexpected explosion of ammunition in the *Hampshire*'s forepart hurled them headlong into the mud. It was only their special steel diving equipment that saved them from death.

'Though temporarily unnerved by their experience, the divers stuck at the task, working with oxygen-acetylene cutting apparatus, and finally succeeded in raising a quantity of documents, books and £10,000 worth of gold to the surface in small airtight metal caskets.

'. . . they actually put into Stromness for the week-end. Each diver and sailor was sworn to secrecy by the captain, but it was not until some days later that they resumed the operations that resulted in the divers' injuries and forced an immediate dash to Konigsberg.'

By December 1933 the story had been given in such elaborate detail in the German, American and British press that the Admiralty issued the following statement:

'The *Hampshire* belongs to Britain and before anyone can begin salvage of her it is necessary to enter into a contract with the Admiralty.

'If these salvage operations are proved to be going on, or to have been carried out, they are definitely illegal, and action will be taken against the people concerned.

'This information is new to us, and we must now wait until this salvage ship sails again from Germany to continue her work in the Pentland Firth. Then we shall take the necessary steps to stop their operations unless some agreement is arrived at.'

The day after this 'statement' was issued, the Admiralty officially informed the *Morning Post*: 'The Admiralty knows nothing about the matter at all and has issued no statement.'

Yet the statement previously quoted was quite definitely made by an Admiralty spokesman two days before, to the *Sunday Chronicle*, which printed it.

I have carefully sifted through all published stories of this salvage attempt, and, apart from what has already been mentioned, these 'facts' emerge:

(1) The three divers made their last attempt on April 24, 1933;

(2) The diver Whitefield said he received a 'mysterious telegram' at the beginning of 1933, summoning him without explanation to London. An impressively substantial advance of money persuaded him to go. From London he was directed to Southampton, from the latter port to Hamburg and Kiel, where he was instructed to report to 'the captain of a salvage vessel flying the British flag'.

(3) Whitefield was not told of the salvage plans until the ship reached Stromness.

(4) A lifeboat, some broken furniture and a piano floated to the surface after the time-bombs had been exploded by the salvage party.

Nothing more was heard of this incredible feat until in 1951 a book entitled *Unlocking Adventure* by the locksmith, Charles Courtney, was published. This repeated in even greater detail the original story supposed to have been told by the diver Whitefield.

But Courtney gave some interesting additional information. He told how he had come into contact with Frederick Krupp, president of the Krupp shipbuilding plant at Kiel, and Johan George Stein, with whom he had worked out the Stein-Krupp method of submarine gold-mining. Through Krupp he met Sir Basil Zaharoff and several other international financiers who were interested in 'undersea hunting'.

Sir Basil Zaharoff invited Courtney to Biarritz, where 'in confidence he told me that a syndicate of which he was a member had discovered the wreck of H.M.S. *Hampshire*'. According to Zaharoff the cruiser had not only been carrying the War Minister to Russia, but gold to bolster the Czar's wavering army.

'That gold was what they were after—£2 million in bullion of the Bank of England. The currents were strong off Orkney, and the weather difficult. Already a sandsucker was at work, digging at the eight feet of sand that buried part of the wreck, and the salvaging could begin in the spring as soon as the weather permitted.'

Courtney mentioned Costello—'a lanky Australian who had brought up gold from many a famous wreck'—but his story differed in one important detail from the original. He made no mention of Whitefield, but spoke of 'Mansfield' from Norfolk, Virginia, 'one of the best divers on the eastern coast, like his father before him'.

Courtney somewhat vaguely referred to the salvage vessel as the 'K.S.R., a stout, snub-nosed' craft, and gave the name of the captain as Brandt. He confirmed that this German ship wore the British flag for the purposes of the expedition and had a crew comprised of Greeks, Cypriots and Italians. Mention was also made of two other individuals—a diver named Gruber and Max Weissfelt, 'a stout, middle-aged German who said he represented the syndicate'.

Technically, the descriptions of the diving operations were realistic and plausible and Courtney gave the minutest details of the descent to the wreck. All divers wore armoured suits to withstand the high pressure expected. 'At 385 feet there was light enough to see our way around. The fine sand that our boots stirred made the water thick and murky, like a fog,' he wrote.'

'Every gun on the cruiser was loaded and beside it was a mound of skeletons with earphones on their heads, lying by shells that were never fired. These men had not deserted their stations.

'In the forward hatch we stumbled over hundreds of skeletons, sailors who had tried to come up from below deck when the order was given to abandon ship.'

Detailed and realistic as this book is, it is riddled with inaccuracies and inconsistencies, of which the two preceding paragraphs provide an example. The guns' crews aboard the *Hampshire* would only be closed up at their turrets if 'action stations' had been sounded. No such order had been given. As the author admits—and as the survivors testified—the last order was 'abandon ship', which makes the 'skeletons with earphones' narrative a piece of nonsense.

The author also made the error of repeating hearsay without checking up on his facts. He retold the story of the deciphering officer at Neumunster, claiming that one of the salvage vessel's officers had heard it from the man who intercepted the message. But Courtney not only got the date of this wrong —June 1 instead of May 27—but gave the number of Beitzen's U-boat as U57 instead of U75, and then asserted that this submarine laid the mines on June 2 and was back at his base in Heligoland on the following day!

Max Weissfelt was supposed to have been in the German Navy during World War I and to have kept a notebook recording where each German mine was laid. After the war, by comparing his notebook with German naval records, he pinpointed the exact position where the *Hampshire* must have sunk. Then, with an Englishman named Henry Row, he spent three years dragging the waters off Marwick Head before locating the wreck, an effort which does not say much for his chartwork, his navigation or his seamanship. But even this story is ruined by fondness for melodrama; there is a description of how Weissfelt went down in a diving suit and 'brought up a piece of the vessel that was lettered H.M.S. *Hampshire*'!

Yet Courtney at least gave an answer to the question posed at the beginning of the chapter. As to whether the holes in the ship's side were made by a mine or torpedo, he expressed no opinion. Costello, he said, was not sure on this point, but thought the larger hole was undoubtedly made by a mine. 'The small one might have been made by a torpedo that hit on a slant and tore a jagged opening instead of the usual round hole. Of one thing he was positive—there had been no explosion from within as had been rumoured in England.'

Yet this judgement does not sound at all like the considered opinion of an expert. Surely no deep-sea diver, with experience of wrecks in war and peace, would suggest that one hole was made by a mine and the other by a torpedo. And one would also expect an expert to say exactly why there could have been no explosion from within. But Courtney did not even say whether the holes were torn outwards or inwards: one is merely left to assume they were torn inwards.

When the *K.S.R.* returned to Germany, Courtney was delegated to deliver the gold safely into the vaults of the Reichsbank: 'It was April 29. Hjalmar Schacht himself thanked me and invited me to attend the great May Day celebration at which Adolf Hitler was to speak.'

It was on a later trip to Marwick Head that Costello and Courtney were injured on the sea-bed when a cross-current temporarily trapped them. When Courtney looked at himself in a mirror in hospital he saw that his hair 'was completely white'.

When the British press asked the Admiralty for their opinion of this book, they met with the usual non-commital silence: they had 'no official comment to make'.

Charles Courtney died in 1947. He was a locksmith who ran the business of Courtney Lock and Hardware Corporation in the Bronx district of New York. He had an international reputation as an expert on locks and safes, and he was employed in this capacity on various occasions by Sir Basil Zaharoff. The executors of Zaharoff have vouched for the fact that after Zaharoff's death in 1937 Courtney was engaged to open the financier's safes.

But no one seems to have heard of him as a diver.

His business is run today by his son-in-law, Mr. Harold Zippser, but he knows no more about the events mentioned than is contained in his father-in-law's book. He thought the only fresh information available would be in the Zaharoff archives.

How often has one heard the phrase—'the Zaharoff archives'. That sinister international munitions agent, who fomented wars and waxed fat on the proceeds, has baffled all those who have attempted to write his life. Zaharoff's career is still a hotch-potch of fact and self-inspired fiction. One seeks for his birth certificate and learns that 'a fire destroyed the church register'. One looks for a document concerning him in the archives of the War Office at Vienna only to find that the folder is there, but that the document has vanished. Everywhere Zaharoff systematically set out to remove or obliterate evidence of his machinations.

That Zaharoff would be in a position to know whether or not the *Hampshire* was carrying gold to Russia is only too probable. He managed to know everything of importance. Mr. Archibald de Bear, who was at one time Zaharoff's secretary, wrote of the arms king's imbroglios: 'Huge sums were paid regularly for the details of Government plans regarding shipbuilding and armaments construction in general. Authentic information regarding the preparatory plans for Army and Navy estimates often reached Paris . . . deviously, but unfailingly long before being made known in Parliament by the departments concerned.

'The supply of this intelligence came from highly-placed officers of State. They were on the regular pay roll for that purpose and their identities were disguised by code names.'*

Zaharoff worked in the closest co-operation with Lloyd George, both at the Ministry of Munitions and later at 10 Downing Street. 'As a representative of Vickers, Zaharoff was the confidant of Lloyd George, Minister of Munitions, and this personal relationship continued when the latter became Prime Minister,' wrote Richard Lewinssohn. 'In England his best friend was Lloyd George,' claimed Guilles Davenport.

When the name of Zaharoff loomed large and scandalously in the hearings of the Senate Munitions Investigation Commission in Washington in 1934, Mr. Alkin E. Johnson, expounding on the theme in the French review *La Lumière*, said: 'Someone belonging to Lloyd George's more intimate circle told me that "we use Sir Basil Zaharoff as a kind of super-spy in high society and influential circles. At the same time we have him watched by two or three of our best police agents." '

Presumably this referred to the period of Lloyd George's premiership. But, if Zaharoff had the scope for finding out that the *Hampshire* carried gold, why should he, a man worth £40

Sunday Express, November, 1936.

millions at the height of his power, take such trouble and risk so much to steal a mere two millions from the wreck?

There are two possible answers. First, Zaharoff had an almost pathological love of mystery. Perhaps a life of intrigue had left him a lonely old man with nothing more to intrigue about, and, as a compensation, he indulged in fantastic day dreams. Perhaps, as a grim jest, he invented the story of the salvaging of the cruiser. He fooled many people with similarly fantastic stories. There is also the possibility, though this seems unlikely, that he invented the whole episode as a cover for some other hunt for under-water treasure.

But the *Abwehr* had another theory. According to Herr Stoermer, Zaharoff offered the Nazi leaders to finance an expedition to recover gold from the *Hampshire* on the understanding that the *Abwehr* would return to him a dossier on his activities in World War I. This was late in 1932, when world opinion was extremely adverse to Zaharoff and when he had cause to fear alarming disclosures by governmental inquiries into the munitions industry.

At the end of 1916, shortly after he became Premier, Lloyd George asked Zaharoff what were the chances of obtaining unofficially from the enemy a token withdrawal of troops on both sides in selected areas of the Western Front on New Year's Day. This approach was apparently made without the Cabinet being consulted. Zaharoff was at that time seriously perturbed because M. Albert Thomas, French Minister of Munitions, was demanding the bombardment of Briey, close to the German frontier, where, before the war, a series of blast furnaces had been created by the *Comité des Forges*. In August 1914 no attempt had been made to defend Briey, and French forces were immediately withdrawn to a distance of twenty-two kilometres behind the frontier, leaving this valuable industrial plant intact in German hands. Throughout the war no offensive action was taken by the Allies against Briey or nearby Thionville, a German industrial area which was vital to the German army from the point of view of mineral supplies.

Thus it is easy to see why Zaharoff was disturbed at Thomas' demand for the destruction of an arms plant in which he had an interest. So he immediately sought to distort Lloyd George's plea into a plan for a mutual agreement between the Allies and the Central Powers to desist from attacking each other's arms plants. As a result orders to bombard Briey were cancelled.

In the French Parliament on January 24, 1919, M. Barthe testified 'I declare that, either owing to the international solidarity of heavy industry, or in order to safeguard private interests, orders were given to our military commanders not to bombard the factories of the basin of Briey exploited by the enemy during the war.'

M. Barthe compiled a dossier on this sordid episode of the war, and it categorically indicted Zaharoff. This document was suppressed by the French authorities, but a copy was purloined and given to the Nazis.

The details of the document were revealed to me by Herr Stoermer. 'They told of the negotiations between Lloyd George and Zaharoff and made it clear that Lloyd George finally concurred with Zaharoff's viewpoint that it would be senseless to destroy industrial plant and to end the war with derelict factories. He (Lloyd George) was personally in favour of anything that would slow down the tempo of the war on the Western Front and argued that it was better to have the means of supplying arms to the theatre of war that really mattered— vital sectors of the *Moyen-Orient*.

'Zaharoff concurred in this not only because it brought him nearer his life's ambition—the welding of an empire for Greece at the expense of the Central Powers and with Allied aid—but because such a policy would mean more arms orders for his interests. Only Zaharoff stood to gain by such a move. It could have been very embarrassing for him, had German official circles made this public.'

Doubtless this is a somewhat oversimplified statement of a complex situation. But it is worth noting the comment of the

Leipzige Neueste Nachrichten of October 10, 1917: 'If, in the first days of the war, the French had penetrated to the depth of a dozen kilometres in Lorraine, the war could have ended in six months by the defeat of Germany.'

However, these are little more than the 'asides' of history, and, though they may explain Zaharoff's motives for wanting the *Hampshire* to be salvaged, they prove nothing. M. D'Albuquerque, who was also a former secretary of Zaharoff, says 'I have, of course, heard of this story, and I know that M. Zaharoff always insisted that there was a vast quantity of gold in the *Hampshire*. He had discussions on this subject with two prominent German shipbuilders. But I know nothing about the salvage expedition, or whether it even took place.'

I asked the Admiralty whether they could deny or confirm that the cruiser was carrying gold. They gave this reply 'There is no mention in Admiralty records of any shipment of gold being carried to Russia in H.M.S. *Hampshire*.'

This, of course, is not the same thing as positively denying that gold was carried.

But the more one probes the story of the salvage attempt, the less likely it all sounds. Who was 'Whitefield' or 'Mansfield'? Nobody knows either in Germany or U.S.A. Mr. Neil Todhill, the chief diving and salvage authority in Australia, has never heard of Costello. The State Harbour and Marines Department in Australia contains no mention of him in its records. A thorough check on the lists of German merchant navy and coastal shipping captains and divers, kept in the *Seeberufsgenossenschaft* in Hamburg reveals no record of either Brandt or Gruber.

Nor does the name *K.S.R.* appear in any records. An official of the naval section of the German Defence Ministry in Bonn expressed the opinion that the letters could be an abbreviation for *Kuesten See Rettung* (Coastal Sea Rescue Service), with which some vessels in the area are marked. But this doesn't provide a clue.

When the first report of the salvage attempt was published

in 1933, the secretary of the Salvage Association of Britain said 'I cannot believe this report. My association would almost certainly have heard of any salvage operations. So far as I know the *Hampshire* has never been located, and in any case it has always been understood that the water in which she lies is far too deep for salvage operations.'

Mr. E. F. Cox, of Cox and Danks Ltd., the firm which carried out all the salvage operations on the German warships sunk at Scapa Flow, took much the same line. 'It is almost incredible,' he said, 'that any diving could be done in such a treacherous sea as that part of the Pentland Firth where the *Hampshire* is said to have gone down.

'The currents are terrible, and any diver going down to the bed of the sea in that part is taking the biggest risk of his life. There are currents and cross-currents which make such a feat as near impossible as can be.

'The difficulties of diving are so big there that I cannot think of any man venturing down into the bed of the ocean.'

It is surely significant that, though many elderly captains of German salvage ships in Hamburg and Bremen can remember the story of the expedition of 1933, none of them can supply any additional information. Captain Meyer, of the Hamburg salvage firm, Bugsier and Bergungsreederei, like others, thinks that, if any attempt was made, it was not by a German salvage firm, but by a foreign ship specially chartered by Zaharoff.

But on the possibility of any salvage attempt being successful, German expert opinion agrees with the British. As one expert summed it up, 'It would be impossible for a diver to work there because of the depth at which the ship is lying and the rough seas at that point.'

No one in Orkney has ever seen or heard of any salvage attempt—German or British. I have spoken to people who have looked out over these waters every day of their lives and not one of them has ever noticed any vessel of any kind cruising around suspiciously, or anchored near the position where the cruiser sank. There is no information either of any German ship in Stromness harbour during the periods mentioned and, say the inhabitants, they doubt whether a British flag on a foreign ship would have been an effective disguise. 'To fly a British flag on a German salvage craft would be like putting the Rolls-Royce trade mark on a Volkswagen,' said one. 'It wouldn't fool us.'

There is absolute agreement between six local experts that a salvage attempt on the wreck would be well nigh impossible. 'The *Hampshire* sank in forty fathoms of water,' explained one. 'The tide is strong and fairly rapid, often running at five or six knots. Therefore, even with modern salvage methods, the task seems impossible, and it is more than likely that the storms of the last forty years have battered the wreck to pieces.'

Thus the evidence against the salvage expedition story is overwhelming. Why the Admiralty did not flatly deny it at the time I do not know. By explaining why the reports could not be true they could also have answered the question posed at the beginning of this chapter.

Yet I have no doubt that the story told by Courtney has some factual origins. Courtney was not only Zaharoff's locksmith, but he was also, according to Mr. D'Albuquerque, a confidant of the financier. What is factual and what is pure fantasy is another matter. It seems likelier that the story of gold in the *Hampshire* was suggested to Courtney than that he invented it. It is possible that Zaharoff may have believed there was gold in the cruiser and discussed the project with his locksmith. If this were so, however, it would almost certainly have been in the strictest confidence, and Courtney would hardly have retained the financier's trust right until his death if he had invented the salvage story and caused it to be published.

There would appear to be two possibilities. Either Zaharoff deliberately invented the story as a practical joke, or, in order to stir up some international mischief, he personally instigated its publication. It would have been completely in keeping with his character if he had acted either way.

14

The Secret Report

IS there still in existence a secret report on the sinking of the *Hampshire*?

Admiralty spokesmen have made a quite unnecessary mystery of this subject—first by denying its existence, then by admitting it and finally by denying it again. Sir George Arthur's positive statement on the matter has never been refuted and that is, perhaps, the most significant factor. In Parliament there was a grudging admission that Lord Long *might* have offered to show such a report to Kitchener's biographer.

Two pieces of evidence are worth re-examining. First, a footnote in the White Paper stated: 'It has been suggested both in the Press and in questions in the House of Commons that a particular officer of the Glasgow City Police, who was lent at the time to the naval authorities in the Orkneys, was ordered to make inquiries regarding the loss of the *Hampshire* and made a report containing startling information. The authorities who would have been concerned with any such inquiry and report state that there is no foundation for this story and their denial is confirmed by the officer himself, who states that he was not called upon to make any investigation, and did not furnish any report on any matters connected with the loss of the *Hampshire*.'

Secondly, I would refer back to the questions asked in the House of Commons in 1926 by Major Tasker and others.

Major Tasker made the mistake of referring to 'a Scotland Yard official', having made a report, when, in fact, he should have said 'a member of the Glasgow City Police'. Another questioner referred to 'the reports of a Lieutenant Vance'.

Now the White Paper unwittingly supplies the missing link between 'a Scotland Yard official' and 'Lieutenant Vance'. No name is mentioned, but the reference to 'an officer of the Glasgow City Police' is sufficient. For, while the Navy Lists reveal no 'Lieutenant Vance' who could possibly have been concerned in such inquiries, the lists of those serving in the Glasgow City Police during World War I include the name of Detective-Inspector James McGregor Vance. He retired in 1930 with the rank of 'Lieutenant', which is probably why one M.P. believed he must be a naval officer and so addressed his question to the First Lord of the Admiralty.

Working on the theory that Detective-Inspector Vance must be the officer to whom the White Paper referred, I decided to check up on this officer's activities. Unfortunately Detective-Inspector Vance died in 1937, so there is no possibility of seeking his personal evidence. Even if he were alive today, one must assume that the Official Secrets Act would still preclude him from talking freely.

Despite this, there is sufficient evidence of his activities during World War I from unofficial sources for one to dismiss the footnote in the White Paper as an unreliable and at best misleading statement. Early in World War I Detective-Inspector Vance was seconded from Glasgow for special duties with the Admiralty and he was stationed in Kirkwall.

There is no doubt at all about this. Police records show that it was to the Admiralty and no other department of State that he was seconded. He was well-known in Orkney and highly respected. He was also regarded in his own Police Force and in Admiralty circles as a thoroughly reliable, discreet and efficient officer. Some of his work was connected with counter-espionage and one of his tasks was to keep a close watch on any visitors to Orkney who seemed to be behaving suspiciously. It is no exaggeration to say that he was the most valuable link the Admiralty had in that area with all that was going on in civilian life.

In 1926, shortly after Sir George Arthur wrote to *The Times* about the secret report which Lord Long had offered to show him, someone remembered that Vance had been in Orkney in June 1916, and recalled certain inquiries he had made at that time. Though nothing about this was published, one newspaper reporter heard the rumours and called on Vance. Quite naturally and properly, he refused to discuss the matter.

Officialdom was worried nevertheless. For shortly afterwards Vance was questioned by the Chief Constable of Glasgow and the Lord Provost. Why these people should question him about the *Hampshire* is not at all clear. It in no way concerned either of them, and Vance, taking this view, maintained the same silence as towards the newspaper reporter. Doubtless the Chief Constable, as his superior officer, was anxious to know whether Vance had been talking to anyone and making improper disclosures. But it can be most emphatically stated that the rumours did not emanate from Vance who, to the end of his days, kept silent on the subject.

Confirmation that Vance made inquiries into events connected with the sinking of the *Hampshire* comes from several sources. People in Orkney, whom he questioned at the time, are still alive. The late Admiral Sir Guy Gaunt told me: 'There is no doubt at all that Detective-Inspector Vance personally submitted a report to the Admiralty. But it does not follow that this report was ever released from secret papers. It may even have been destroyed.

'Alternatively, there is this possibility: if Vance's inquiries led him to discoveries which were not directly concerned with the actual sinking of the cruiser, the authorities could have decided that his report should be omitted from the official dossier on the subject.'

Admiral Gaunt—the 'nautical Sherlock Holmes', the Americans called him—had a distinguished record in intelligence work as his triumphs in counter-espionage against Count Bernstorf and Captain Boy-Ed bear testimony. He was a gallant, bluff, uncompromising man in the Roger Keyes tradition and he did not suffer fools or fainthearts gladly. In consequence he had many enemies, not only in the Admiralty, but in the Foreign Office where his probings and promptings into the efficiency of their own intelligence systems caused many heartburnings even as late as World War II.

Gaunt took the view that some highly placed officers at the Admiralty were so shocked by the *Hampshire* tragedy and so incredulous at first that mines could have been laid on the route the cruiser took that they were inclined to believe sabotage was a possibility. Further, he was convinced that, though they might have been ultimately satisfied that there was no actual sabotage, Vance's evidence probably showed there was an attempt at sabotage. And, in the Admiralty's view, the latter revelation would be almost as damaging to their prestige as the real thing.

While in Washington during World War I, Gaunt learned from an American naval intelligence officer that the Americans had proof of an Irish Republican plot not only to kill Kitchener, but to sabotage British warships as retaliation for the execution of Sir Roger Casement. But the Americans were not anxious to co-operate in providing proofs as they did not wish to 'offend the powerful Irish vote'. For the 'Irish vote', though not numerically powerful except in certain cities, was the symbol of all small nations fighting against great powers and it rallied to its support all other minority communities in U.S.A.

*   *   *   *   *

On the afternoon when the *Hampshire* sailed from Scapa Detective-Inspector Vance's attention was drawn to two seemingly isolated, but rather disturbing items of information. The first was news of the small vessel flying the Dutch flag seen cruising around Marwick Head. Vance, who was in Kirkwall, did not see the vessel, but heard of it from the fisherman, Peddie.

When Vance made further inquiries he learned that the ship had last been seen heading for the open sea in a south-westerly direction. This struck him as being odd because, with such a storm raging, it seemed senseless for a small fishing vessel to venture far away from land. A south-westerly course would take the ship towards the Isle of Lewis, a hazardous voyage in such conditions. Most other vessels had either stayed in har- bour, when the storm cones were hoisted, or were heading for the nearest port. Nobody had thought fit to ascertain what the ship was doing in these parts.

More disturbing, however, was the information that an Irishman, a stranger to the district who was thought to be a seaman, had been seen in Kirkwall. For there was no record of any person answering to his description having landed in Orkney during the previous month.

Vance at first thought this Irishman might be a deserter from the Navy, but the naval authorities had reported no desertions from the Scapa Flow area.

Being a meticulous officer and a painstaking investigator Vance decided to make inquiries on his own account. He did not then know that the N.I.D. had been too preoccupied with the events of Jutland to follow up reports of the Irish Re- publicans' plot to assassinate Kitchener. But he knew enough of I.R.A. activities to realise that the presence of an unidentified Irishman in the vicinity of Scapa Flow could be a serious matter.

The Irishman had made a rendezvous with an Orcadian fisherman for five o'clock on the afternoon of June 5. Detective- Inspector Vance, sipping a cup of tea, was unobtrusively wait- ing at the café where he was expected.

By 5.30 p.m. the Irishman had failed to appear. The waitress in the café remarked rather wistfully 'It's strange he hasn't come back. He promised faithfully to come in and bring me some flowers.'

Many men have made similar promises to pretty girls and failed to fulfil them, but Vance was impressed by the fact that in this instance the fisherman as well as the waitress had been let down.

But it took him a long time to piece together the story of the mysterious Irishman. The Orcadian fisherman was at first sullen and hostile in replying to Vance's patient questions. He did not know anything about the Irishman; come to that, he might not have been an Irishman at all, but he was a good fellow all the same and, if he hadn't turned up, well there must be a good reason for it and nothing for a policeman to get all bothered about. And that was that.

The waitress was more forthcoming. To be sure she had only known the gentleman for a few days—it might have been a week, or rather less—but certain it was that he was Irish. 'There wasn't any mistaking that lovely brogue of his. A really charming gentleman he was. A seaman? Well, yes, that is what he said he was, but he was such a gentleman he might have been anything.'

Detective-Inspector Vance had an idea that the waitress had something more than a soft spot for the Irishman and that the latter had served up a pretty useful line of blarney.

He made other inquiries in Kirkwall, but the fact was that, though the Irishman had talked volubly, and thus disarmed suspicion, he had said very little of importance. Nobody could recall hearing where he had come from. But one thing was certain: the Irishman whom the detective-inspector sought was no phantom, no figment of anyone's imagination. Evidence was taken from at least eight people who had seen him, spoken with him and of whom five were positive that he was not only unmistakeably Irish, but a stranger to the islands. Later the waitress blushingly admitted that he had told her to call him 'Sean' and had given her flowers and a lucky horseshoe as presents.

Then came a clue as to his name. A fisherman remembered that the Irishman had said his nickname was 'Sweeney' because he was ship's barber at sea. Gradually it became apparent that he had told slightly different stories to different people. He had

told some he hadn't been to Ireland for three years; to others
he was a merchant seaman on leave from Belfast, having been
looking up some friends at Thurso, while he explained his
presence in the islands to the waitress by saying he was in
Orkney on a week's holiday.

Probably Vance would not have worried so much about the
Irishman if he had not also received information about the
Dutch fishing vessel. But he had a hunch that in some way the
two incidents were connected. And in Kirkwall these two items
of news, coupled with Vance's inquiries, quickly became common gossip and developed into a minor spy scare just about the
time that the *Hampshire* went down. Not unnaturally this added
to the general panic when news of the cruiser's sinking filtered
through.

As far as the Admiralty were concerned, the *Hampshire*
disaster occurred at the worst possible psychological moment.
Coming so soon after Jutland, when nerves and tempers in
Whitehall were frayed by revelations of the extent to which the
Germans had intercepted British signals, its impact was
shattering. Everyone panicked; from those in charge in the
Admiralty to the naval authorities in Orkney. Fearing the effect
on public opinion of the slightest hint of sabotage or negligence, the most rigorous security measures were ordered. It was
the tense, hyper-sensitive psychological atmosphere which
caused the stupid and irrational behaviour of the naval
authorities in Kirkwall and Stromness and the unintelligent
interpretation of security orders resulted in many lives being
lost.

The *London Gazette* of June 6 announced new restrictions
on passengers landing at ports in Orkney 'no passenger is to
land or embark at any port in the Orkney Isles without permission of the Naval Authority in Kirkwall.'

This was typical of various panic-inspired moves. It would
have been much more sensible to have conducted a rigorous
check on people coming in and out of Orkney without adver-
ising the fact. The publicity given to the *London Gazette*

announcement only created a nation-wide spy scare. The Irish-man, whoever he was, was never found in the islands. He was traced to Dounby and Stromness, but there his trail ended. The last time he was seen at Dounby was on the night of June 4, about twelve hours before Detective-Inspector Vance had first been told of his presence in the islands. A thorough check of all ships which had left Orcadian ports in the previous forty-eight hours was made on June 6, but it seemed certain that the Irish-man could not have departed in any of these.

Could he have got away in the fishing vessel flying the Dutch flag? Here again the evidence is confused. Mr. Fox-Davies mentioned that this craft had been seen 'several days before' June 5. The fisherman, Peddie, who reported the matter to Vance, insisted he had seen the ship 'early on June 5'. Two other eye-witnesses testified to seeing it heading south-west on the morning of that day. But while one thought it was a foreign ship, the other said it was too far out to sea to tell what flag it was flying. Yet another fisherman swore he had seen the vessel some days earlier, that it was a Dutch craft and that he had exchanged greetings with the skipper. It should also be noted that Sir Henry Dalziel's question in the House of Commons re-ferred to its being seen 'immediately before the *Hampshire* reached the spot where she sank'.

In Orkney at the time there was mention of a second Irish-man who had helped the other to escape, but this can be dis-counted as hearsay. Coincidentally, one of the rumours then current bore a remarkable resemblance to Ernst Carl's story. A nurse at the Balfour Hospital in Kirkwall recollected that two survivors from the cruiser received treatment at the hospital. She is still alive and she recalls that there was 'a certain air of mystery surrounding them', but whether this was due to wartime security measures in keeping them apart from other patients she cannot say. But she remembers that they were re-puted to be Irish and that people whispered that they had been able to 'escape from the ship owing to being in the know beforehand'.

It is certain that most of these rumours were wild speculation and very wide of the mark. Doubtless, too, somebody recalled that the nickname of 'Sweeney', claimed by the Irishman,
was the same as the surname of one of the survivors. This may
be the explanation of the unsubstantiated story that one of the
crew was suspected of sabotage. Long afterwards Sweeney was
taunted with being a saboteur, a cruel slander which could well
have played a part in his subsequent mental breakdown.

* * * * *

Towards the end of June 1916 a fishing skipper in the Isle of
Lewis reported having seen an Irishman answering to the description of 'Sean' or 'Sweeney'.

His story was that the Irishman had been landed by rowing
boat from another fishing vessel not far from Stornoway. He
gave his name as O'Connor and spun a yarn about having got
his call-up papers and that therefore he must get to Glasgow
immediately. On the strength of this story he secured a passage
with the fishing skipper to Oban.

Probably the fishing skipper would have thought no more
about this incident, but for the fact that when he arrived at
Oban, the Irishman, instead of travelling to Glasgow by land,
asked whether he could get there by boat. As he had originally
stressed that he must report to Glasgow within forty-eight
hours of his arrival in Oban, the skipper thought this distinctly
odd. The Irishman must have suspected that the skipper did not
believe his story, for he vanished shortly afterwards without
saying good-bye.

On the strength of this report Detective-Inspector Vance
made inquiries in Oban. Mrs. Alice Maclean was able to confirm his suspicions that this Irishman and the man seen in
Orkney were one and the same. He came into her shop to buy
newspapers and he particularly asked for copies of any back
numbers for the first two weeks of June.

'I'm sorry, but I'm afraid we haven't any left,' she told him,
'though we can get you them. Is there any special paper you
want? Or is it something special you are looking for?'

'No, it doesn't matter,' was the reply. 'I have been away at sea for a week or so and I'm out of touch with the news. I just wondered whether anything big had happened.'

'Well,' said Mrs. Maclean, 'I suppose you have heard all about Lord Kitchener's death and the *Hampshire* disaster?'

. The Irishman stood motionless for a moment. 'He seemed quite shocked and bewildered,' said Mrs. Maclean, 'so I told him all about it. He obviously hadn't heard, but I had a feeling that he was more than just shocked. He looked at me as though he was frightened of something, as though he mistrusted me. Then he asked me what was the date on which the *Hampshire* sank. When I told him he kept repeating it "June the fifth, June the fifth".'

Despite this evidence, there was really very little on which Vance could work. Indeed, but for his two errors in Oban, the Irishman would probably not have been traced as far as there. And, having realised his errors, he covered up his tracks by promptly vanishing again.

The skipper of the fishing smack could not confirm the identity of the fishing vessel from which the Irishman was put ashore. He felt sure it wasn't flying the Dutch flag, but in every other respect, even down to the details of the wireless equipment it carried, it was similar to that described by Peddie. No one else in Lewis had taken much notice of the vessel; it was assumed that the craft had anchored some distance off Stornoway after a severe buffeting in the storm. It never put into port and shortly after the Irishman landed sailed away again.

No one answering to the Irishman's description reported at any military barracks or call-up centre in the Glasgow area. Thus the scant evidence available to Detective-Inspector Vance suggests that 'Sean' had something to hide. His story to the skipper of the Lewis fishing smack was quite different from anything he told in Orkney. He did not pretend he was a merchant seaman, but said he had been to sea with his father-in-law who, owing to the war, was short of deck hands.

Whether Vance, who by all accounts pursued his inquiries

on these matters for many months, discovered anything further only the secret report could reveal. But the story of the mysterious Irishman tallies with that of the Sinn Feiner told by Frank Ryan. Unfortunately, by the time I learned the details given in this chapter, Ryan was dead, so there was no opportunity to make a further check. I have no reason to doubt what Ryan told me; he was one of the most honest men I ever came across, and, though a former Chief of Staff of the I.R.A., was not anti-British. Indeed, for resolving to renounce violence and deciding to pursue a strictly democratic political path, he was reviled and threatened with death by the extremists of the I.R.A. Even then—in the mid-thirties—some of the latter were prepared to do a deal with Nazi Germany. But not Ryan. He went to Spain to fight on the Republican side against the German and Italian legionaries.

But Ryan had no personal knowledge of these events. He had only passed on what he had heard from the Sinn Feiner. Therefore, reluctantly, one must treat his testimony with reserve. Yet the fact that he mentioned an Irishman escaping from Orkney by way of Lewis must in itself be something more than mere coincidence. This would not have been a normal escape route.

* * * * *

There have been suggestions that spies got away from the *Hampshire* by one of the cruiser's boats. These are quite ridiculous and can be dismissed at once.

Apart from this, a story persisted for many years that Kitchener and Lieutenant-Colonel Fitzgerald left the cruiser together in one of the boats. In the House of Commons on February 10, 1926, Sir Robert Hamilton asked the First Lord whether he was aware that the small boat in which the War Minister and his military secretary left the *Hampshire* had been purchased by a private individual and whether this boat could be acquired by the Admiralty as a national relic.

Mr. Bridgeman replied 'I shall be obliged if the honourable

and gallant gentleman will repeat his question in a week's time, when I hope the inquiries will be complete.'

Nothing came of this inquiry, but the facts about the *Hampshire*'s boats are indisputable and uncomplicated. The shore parties discovered an empty smashed cutter in Skaill Bay on the morning of June 6; the *Flying Kestrel* sighted the carvel-built pinnace when she was nearing Stromness on her return to harbour, this boat being subsequently taken into Longhope (fragments of it were later sent to the Imperial War Museum); the *Jason II* saw a whaler or galley which was broken amidships, but the weather was too rough to pick up the pieces. This may have been the Captain's boat, as a cap, bearing the name of Captain Savill, was picked up in the vicinity. A 30-foot whaler was washed ashore in Thurso Bay; it contained no bottom boards and parts of the bow were missing.

The only mystery regarding the boats is contained in this statement in the White Paper 'The sixteen-foot dinghy (clinker-built) has passed into private possession and been exhibited (in London). Its history remains uncertain. This was the smallest boat in the ship. It was in the *Hampshire* certainly until the end of May, 1916. The captain then asked for it to be replaced—for what reason it is impossible now to say—and a new one was ordered from Devonport, but never reached the ship. Whether after being thus marked out for replacement, the dinghy was actually carried in the *Hampshire* on June 5 is not quite certain. During the war boats of small size were, in such circumstances, 'dumped' on shore. There is no reference to it in the narrative of any survivor. If it was on board it would normally have been stowed amidships near the floats and may have floated clear and been broken up on the rocks, but there is no evidence as to this.

'Efforts to attach special importance to this boat as a relic of the *Hampshire* have led its present owner into a ludicrous identification of the pieces of a carvel-built boat in the Imperial War Museum as the missing portion of this sixteen-foot clinker skiff dinghy. On the impossibility of this identification of two boats so different in size and construction being pointed out, an attempt has been made to pretend that the missing portion of the dinghy is or was at one time in the Royal United Services Institution Museum, but the authorities of that Museum state definitely that they have never had any portion of an ex-*Hampshire* boat there.'

The so-called *Hampshire* boat was exhibited at premises in Oxford Street during 1926. Shipwright Phillips visited the exhibition and declared positively that it was not one of the cruiser's boats. He also saw there 'a specimen of my own hand-writing and a photograph of me'. He had no idea how these souvenirs were obtained; they were certainly not shown with his permission.

The White Paper says 'there is no evidence of any other identified boats or fragments of boats'. This is incorrect. Many such relics were obtained privately and are still in existence. Detective-Inspector Vance had among his most cherished pos-sessions a walking-stick made from an oar of one of the *Hamp-shire*'s boats. The present Lord Kitchener has in his possession a cigarette-box made from a boat of the *Hampshire*, which was given to him by his father.

In a letter, dated May 14, 1919, Captain Reginald C. Lloyd Owen, R.N., wrote to Viscount Broome 'I would be very pleased if you would accept the enclosed box, which was made from the timbers of the ship's boat of H.M.S. *Hampshire*, in which Lord Kitchener lost his life. The boat was washed up on the Orkney coast the day after the *Hampshire* was lost, and was brought into Stromness Harbour.

'The piece of timber was given to me by the Senior Naval Officer, Stromness, at the time of the disaster. I feel sure this relic will be of interest to the Kitchener family.'

Wreckage from the boats was washed up more than 100 miles from Marwick Head. In view of the fact that a reward of £100 had been offered for the recovery of Lord Kitchener's dispatch case and that it was known that many important papers and books in the ship might not have been destroyed before the sinking, immense carelessness was shown in rounding up the fragments from the wreck. A chest of drawers and other pieces of furniture were said to have been washed ashore and bought by a private person. The relief party which went out from Stromness on June 6 actually saw the chest of drawers and other articles washed up on the beach, yet failed to do anything to retrieve them. When they returned later, the articles had disappeared. 'This property appears to have been wrongfully removed,' commented the White Paper.

This incident was one of many investigated by Detective-Inspector Vance. An Aberdonian who found a wooden box containing certain papers while fishing off the north-eastern tip of Caithness late in June 1916, sold it as a souvenir to a Glasgow merchant. The latter happened to mention this later to an acquaintance who informed the police. In due course the merchant was asked to give Vance a detailed explanation of how he came to acquire this relic.

Doubtless, but for the unfortunate publicity which it would have caused, the merchant would have been prosecuted, but as the souvenir proved to be nothing more than a sailor's ditty box containing a bundle of old newspapers and personal letters, no serious harm was done.

Indeed in this instance perhaps it was as well that no effort was made to return the box and its contents to the sailor's widow. For the letters were obviously from 'another woman'.

But though unauthorised persons obtained souvenirs of the wreck, and though few of them were traced, suggestions that papers from the cruiser fell into the hands of enemy agents can be discounted. There is no evidence to support this.

15

Verdict on Six Counts

IN telling this complicated story, the main problem has been to decide what evidence to reject. I have taken the view that this is something which the reader rather than the author ought to decide. And, though I may be accused of having lured the reader up some very unprofitable blind alleys in a quest for facts which have not always proved relevant, I feel that at least he is now in a position to draw his own conclusions.

Even the most far-fetched theories and statements have been closely examined. To have ignored them would have been a mistake, rather like hastily brushing old love letters under the carpet and thereby creating an unnecessary atmosphere of mystery. Not even the Admiralty could afford to ignore every wild *canard*, as the detailed sifting of the Belfast spy scare in White Paper Cmd. 2710 shows. But the Admiralty carefully selected the more fantastic allegations and proceeded to debunk them, while completely ignoring other questions which demanded an answer. Then again, the Admiralty issued the White Paper largely to refute the allegations of one man—Frank Power—who had already been largely discredited. And the White Paper is very far from being the last word in this affair, for the detailed allegations of sabotage and interception of signals were made long after the White Paper was published.

By carefully selecting some material and rejecting other evidence, it is possible to give not one, but many different answers to questions which, to date, have not been dealt with by officialdom. The story of the *Hampshire* provides a classical example of how history can be distorted by a prejudiced selection of material. Imagine an historian in A.D. 2000 discovering the works of Bley, or reading the extravagant claims of Fritz Duquesne. He might easily persuade himself that the *Hampshire* was not sunk by a mine. There is no comparable disaster of the same magnitude in modern times which has aroused such intense controversy and speculation, or to which a final solution has seemed so elusive. But, if one takes into account all the evidence given in the preceding chapters, it seems reasonable to accept these conclusions:

(1) That the *Hampshire* was sunk by one or more mines laid by the submarine U75;

(2) That there was carelessness and negligence not only regarding security measures to keep the Russian Mission a secret, but in the sailing arrangements;

(3) That there was an interception of British signals by the German intelligence and that this led to the mining of the waters off Marwick Head;

(4) That stupidity was shown by the Naval authorities in hindering rescue operations both on land and sea, with the result that there was far greater loss of life than need have occurred.

Despite these errors, which could have been avoided, an extraordinary combination of ill luck and coincidence mainly brought about the disaster.

The Admiralty rejected all these conclusions except the first, in which they concur, and the third, on which they have made no comment.

There remain two other possible conclusions. I will put them in question form:

(1) Was there a secret report on these events which has never been revealed?

(2) Was there an I.R.A. plot against Kitchener, and was it the knowledge that an Irish agent, or agents, had penetrated to

Orkney that was in part responsible for the rigid security measures taken after the disaster and the hostility and suspicion so unjustifiably shown towards the Orcadians?

By implication two First Lords answered the first question in the affirmative, while the White Paper emphatically rejected the idea of a secret report. Weighing up this contradictory official evidence with that given by independent witnesses, it is hard to come to any other conclusion than that there must at some time have been in existence a secret report. Equally it seems certain that Detective-Inspector Vance made his own reports to the authorities.

What one cannot be sure of is whether Vance's reports were quite separate from the main secret report, whether they formed part of it or the whole of it. From the last chapter it certainly would not seem that his inquiries alone could have served as the basis of a weighty, comprehensive report. Then again, it would be unusual for a detective-inspector, who had merely been loaned to the Admiralty, to be given such a major task.

But if Vance's inquiries were purely routine, why was there an attempt to pretend he had nothing whatever to do with these events? In the light of his discoveries in Orkney it would seem that, from the Admiralty point of view, Vance had accidentally come across something very far removed from a routine inquiry.

The Admiralty has not given an answer to the second question because until now it has never been raised in any positive form. It is, in fact, the one possibility which has always been overlooked.

These two questions are interlinked, and for this reason they deserve further examination. One of the greatest handicaps in arriving at the truth has been the reluctance of the few survivors still living to talk about the disaster and the fact that on many vital points they are unable to give satisfactory replies. The question of the Official Secrets Act arises, and the fact that they have not been freed from the vow of secrecy which they made at the Naval Court of Inquiry. Thirty years ago, when there were more of these survivors still alive, some of them made anonymous statements to independent researchers and this led to wild and unsubstantiated allegations. One survivor was threatened with prosecution, yet another was told he might lose his pension if he made any further similar statements.

In fairness to these men one must point out that in at least two cases they were exploited by an unscrupulous sensationalist who did not hesitate to distort their remarks for his own ends. They were quoted out of context and many things they did not say were interpolated into their statements. Two other survivors had been subjected to ruthless cross-examination when still suffering from mental strain after the tragedy, and their account of what happened was to some extent coloured by hallucinations. One man was regarded as a hostile witness because he did not hesitate to criticise the handling of the rescue operations.

In the narrative of these events I have only included statements by survivors which are unquestionably theirs and which can be corroborated by independent witnesses. I have excluded all second-hand statements alleged to have been made by survivors, or given anonymously. Two survivors refused to talk.

I quote from one survivor who declined to have his name mentioned, not to present fresh evidence, but to show how misleading such statements can be and how confusing they are, especially after a lapse of more than forty years:

'All my life since June, 1916, I have tried to forget that awful day. I am sorry, but I just do not want to talk about the sinking of the *Hampshire*. Even now I can hardly bear to think about it. In any case my memory is not good and I am not sure I can recall anything, even if I wanted to do so.'

Yet, having made this assertion, the survivor surprisingly added 'There are two things I can never forget. I remember Petty Officer Sweeney saying afterwards that if a water-tight door hadn't been left open, the ship need not have sunk. I can't say which door this was, but Sweeney was most definite about it.

'After we were hit Captain Savill must have been so taken up with getting Lord Kitchener fixed up in one of the boats that he neglected to give the alarm. There was a battery-operated auxiliary wireless transmitting set aboard and there would have been time to send a message for help. But nothing was done.'

To include such a statement as evidence would be pointless. The rating may have been quite right, but he has no proof that Captain Savill failed to give the alarm. It could easily be that the Captain's orders were not carried out.

All available German records have been consulted. But Dr. Erwin Weiss, the Director of the World War Library at Stuttgart, writes 'In my opinion the British Admiralty carried out further investigations after 1916 on the basis of documents captured in Germany.'

This view is supported by Herr Stoermer and others in Germany. Herr Stoermer insists that the *Abwehr* records included new evidence of the *Hampshire* disaster compiled in the 'thirties.

There are conflicting reports about the German Admiralty records of World War I. Some of them are held by the British Admiralty. Fritz Hesse, who was the Nazi press attaché under Herr von Ribbentrop in London and was later a correspondent of the *Volkischer Beobachter*, says that records and documents in Potsdam, which might have contained vital information about the episode, were destroyed by bombing in 1945. Other documents of the German Admiralty were confiscated by the Americans and the Russians. Some of the papers taken by the Soviet have recently been returned to the *Deutsches Zentralarchiv* at Potsdam and Merseburg, but, as far as one can ascertain, there is nothing of value in these.

Professor Kluge, of the Institute of Modern History in Munich, says that most of the *Abwehr* records of World War I were destroyed and that the remainder fell into American hands and have not been returned. He, too, insists that Britain has important German naval records from both world wars.

But I doubt whether there is any more useful information from German sources that has not already been quoted in this

L.K.D.—O

book. All German war historians to whom I have spoken say that the ultimate answer can only come from British sources. There is absolute agreement among them that they do not possess all the facts. Indeed, the allegations of sabotage which are still made by quite intelligent German experts and the conviction that certain highly placed people in Britain wanted Kitchener out of the way are largely due to the reticence of the British Admiralty. The silence of the latter on so many points helped to fan German suspicions that there was something to hide. This is why many Germans in positions of authority refused to believe that the leakages of information from the British side regarding the Russian Mission were not due to some diabolical plot by the British Secret Service.

When it comes to intelligence work, the German mind seems to lose much of its efficiency and clear-headedness and becomes extraordinarily naive and susceptible to all kinds of irrelevant and external influences. Trained to think in the abstract, the German intelligence officer often becomes obsessed with romantic and extravagant abstractions. Thus Himmler was convinced that the Boy Scout movement, Toc H and the Rosicrucians were adjuncts of the British Secret Service!* Ludendorff suffered from similar aberrations.

Herr Stoermer, however, showed commendable logic in disposing of the suggestions that the Germans deliberately and in in detail planned to kill Kitchener during his voyage to Russia. 'Doubtless, as a result of what we learned, a watch for vital transports was kept,' he said. 'Possibly that was borne in mind when the signal was intercepted. But it is still obvious that, even if we had known every detail of the sailing (which we didn't), it would have been far simpler to let Kitchener go to Russia and kill him there. Russian security was hopelessly inefficient and nothing would have been easier than to organise his assassination either in Archangel or Petrograd. As far as we could see—and this was indeed a stupid blunder by the British—your people were relying entirely on the Russians to

*H. R. Trevor-Roper.

provide adequate protection for the War Minister. There was only one detective in Lord Kitchener's party, and he had no knowledge of Russian police methods, nor did he speak Russian. Had Kitchener lived to reach Russia, it is highly probable that he would have been assassinated just the same.'

I asked Herr Stoermer how he knew so much about the detective in the Russian Mission party. He was vague about this, but said he remembered that some such comments had been made when the inquiries into the sinking of the cruiser were re-opened. 'There was a dossier on every member of the party. But I think this information was obtained some years after the sinking.'

While the Nazis ordered the re-opening of these inquiries shortly before the publication of Ernst Carl's *One Against England*, they already knew the outline of his story, as it was then being considered as the basis for a film. Herr Stoermer was quite certain that the proposals for this film had 'raised certain queries in the minds of the authorities, as the Nazis were keenly interested in Carl's narrative and especially in the suggestion of an Irish plot to kill Kitchener.'

It was Herr Stoermer who provided a few clues towards answering the two final conclusions which I posed as questions earlier in this chapter. 'Apparently the information we received originally about the Irish plot had either been destroyed or filed away and forgotten. Our own agents had known all about this plot, but had not taken it seriously as they thought the Irish had not the organisation to carry it out. And it would seem that this view was largely correct.

'Carl's story, however, intrigued the Nazis and they wanted to know more. I think they were impressed by the possibility of the I.R.A. being better organised in the arts of sabotage than Colonel Nicolai's reports suggested. They did not trust his information and insisted on probing further. My own view is that they believed the trail might lead them to Irishmen whom they could use as agents.'

*   *   *   *   *

By the mid-thirties the Nazis' interest in probing the *Hampshire* story was obviously not for historical reasons. The pattern of their activities soon became clear. First Carl's book was banned, then Carl himself was shadowed by the Gestapo. Then *Abwehr II* (Sabotage and Subversion Division) took up the trail. Clearly the Nazi aim was to track down all I.R.A. men who had either co-operated with the Germans in World War I, or had launched deliberate acts of sabotage against Britain. By blackmail and blandishments, they hoped to win new allies in Eire and thus form a 'minorities branch' of *Abwehr II*, aimed solely at recruiting potential Quislings from the various national minorities in the British Isles.

As far as Eire was concerned, however, the Germans soon found that there were not many, even among the extremists of the I.R.A. who were disposed to throw in their lot with Nazi Germany. It soon became evident that their only hope was to find somebody whom they could compromise.

The re-opening of the *Hampshire* inquiries by the *Abwehr* made this possible in the case of one man. From records of World War I in Colonel Nicolai's offices a list was obtained of some twenty-four Irishmen who had been contacted by German agents. By careful elimination they narrowed this down to some half a dozen or so who might have had something to do with the alleged plot against Kitchener.

'Finally,' said Herr Stoermer, 'we found our man. In 1936 we discovered in Cardiff the son of the man who had escaped from Orkney to Lewis and then back to the Scottish mainland. He had changed his name to Griffiths, but admitted to our agent that his real name was Gallagher.

'Naturally he was astounded that we had tracked him down and, in the circumstances, we had little difficulty in persuading him to co-operate with us. From him we learned that his father had been killed by the British auxiliaries in Ireland in 1920, and that fact made him not unnaturally strongly anti-British.

'From what he told us and from what we had already

learned there was no longer any doubt that there was an Irish plot to kill Kitchener. The War Minister had been shadowed by the I.R.A. for some weeks, while at the same time there was a plan under way to sabotage British warships at Scapa Flow by planting time bombs in them. Gallagher was a member of the latter organisation and had been to the Orkneys to keep watch.

'Somehow the Irish had learned about the Russian mission and knew that Kitchener was going north. They had even obtained details of the special train he was catching from King's Cross. It was the Irish who managed to decoy the servant of Mr. O'Beirne of the Foreign Office to Marylebone Station on the pretext that he was to meet a Colonel Datchett there. Knowing that this servant was carrying the ciphers, they hoped in this way to delay Kitchener's journey with the object of gaining time to tip off Gallagher. Presumably they hoped to link up with Gallagher's organisation and assassinate the War Minister at Scapa Flow, or perhaps at Thurso. But events moved too fast for them. Kitchener's journey was not delayed and so there was not time to make any new plans.'

Thus the incidents of 1916 found an echo in World War II and history began to repeat itself. Griffiths, or Gallagher, became a German agent. Whether blackmail or blandishments succeeded in this case one cannot say. His name appears in the *Abwehr II* list of contacts.

Gallagher returned to Eire early in 1939. He was one of the first men to be contacted by the German agent, Hauptmann Goerz, who landed in Eire in 1940 with the aim of establishing an espionage network with the I.R.A. Goerz was working for the 'minorities section' of *Abwehr II*, but he was out of luck from the start. Not only was he arrested and kept in custody until after the war, but as the prospects of a German invasion of the British Isles receded, so the Germans themselves lost interest in the activities of the 'minorities section'.

An entry in *Abwehr* records dated January 28, 1940, refers to the sending of a German agent to Eire 'by submarine U37

. . . to establish contact with Griffiths and arrange for a courier from Dublin to New York through Vertrauensmann (secret agent) "Rex".'

Inquiries both in Britain and in Germany thus confirm that there was an I.R.A. plot against Kitchener, though the details remain vague. But the security measures taken immediately after the *Hampshire* disaster and the closer check on visitors to Orkney must have successfully prevented any further I.R.A. attempts against ships in Scapa. It might even be that the sinking of the cruiser focused the attention of the authorities on the new peril from Ireland.

Undoubtedly, too, Detective-Inspector Vance's inquiries were concerned with the I.R.A. plot.

June 5, 1916, was a day of crisis in more ways than one in the British Admiralty. The surprising efficiency of the Germans' naval intelligence was revealed. Many of the enemy's intelligence ruses and the methods by which they obtained their information were known to Admiral Hall, the head of N.I.D. But Hall, a ruthless autocrat, had not always seen fit to pass on all he knew to his superiors at the Admiralty. For Hall had not a high opinion of some of the Naval commanders. He had actively intrigued against a move to bring back the discredited 'Jacky' Fisher and he had long thought that Jellicoe should be superseded.

Jutland brought matters to a head. As a result of information gained from the battle and through the interception of enemy signals it was clear that the Germans had obtained accurate details of the movements of the Grand Fleet and that the British code for reporting mine clearances was known to the enemy.

Hall had not only known about this before, but had laid traps for enemy submarines on the strength of it. Yet, if he had stressed this danger, the *Hampshire* might never have been sunk. Perhaps Hall was to blame for keeping information to himself, though he could reasonably argue that successful counter-espionage often depended upon commanders-in-chief and other senior officers not knowing exactly what he was doing.

In the days after Jutland, Beatty, a man of action who had little time for those in Whitehall, was scathing in his indictment of 'the inefficiency of Admiralty signals'. He complained that he could not trust them, as, three hours after he had received one such message, telling him that the German Fleet was in harbour, he met the whole Fleet at sea! But this was an unfair and sweeping criticism, for the fault was not that of the N.I.D., but of an inexperienced Operations officer who confused the call signs.

'One of the strangest features of the battle (Jutland) was that the British Admiralty knew Jellicoe's disposition for the night from German Admiralty signals deciphered in Room 40,' wrote Admiral Sir William James. 'Very soon after Jellicoe had signalled his destroyers to take station astern for the night, the German Admiralty repeated the signal to von Scheer. This was a remarkable performance because, owing to our practice of breaking wireless silence only when absolutely necessary, the German cryptographers were starved of material.'*

Thus there was for some days a distorted picture of what was going on. Both Beatty and Jellicoe blamed the Admiralty for inadequate or inaccurate information. There was a widespread belief in some naval circles that British naval intelligence had been completely fooled by the Germans and a real fear that the Germans had obtained far more of our secrets than was in fact the case. Hall was blamed for everything that went wrong at Jutland, which was most unjust. Hall in turn blamed the Admiralty for treating his beloved Room 40 as a cell for amateur cryptographers who were not allowed to pass on their own comments on signals to Operations.

In this way the lack of co-operation between the Naval Intelligence Division and the Operations Division of the

*The Eyes of the Navy. Otto Kruger referred to the wireless silence of British ships and said that, knowing of this security black-out, the intercepted signal from a British destroyer was considered especially important.

Admiralty was spotlighted. While the Battle of Jutland revealed blunders caused by misinterpretation of enemy signals, the inquiries which followed the sinking of the cruiser showed up a whole chapter of signalling errors, failure to co-ordinate information and slack organisation. Admiral Hall won his point that the professors and schoolmasters who had been deciphering enemy signals in Room 40 were fully qualified to transfer these signals into intelligence reports. Indeed, by their experience of the almost imperceptible changes in wireless traffic which often preceded some new enemy move, they were better qualified than the naval officers in Operations Division.

Perhaps Hall was lucky. For if the implications of the telltale signal intercepted by the Germans had been fully weighed, he might well have been held responsible for this blunder. Instead he chose offence rather than defence as the best weapon. Within a few months his staff was increased and the decipherers were given the task of preparing intelligence summaries. It was an immense step forward and one which was to prove a factor of incalculable value in winning the war. For the civilians in Room 40 quickly proved that they could assimilate a remarkably diverse assortment of information, and, in sifting material containing political implications, they were more competent to make accurate assessments. By the end of 1917 British naval intelligence was far in advance of any similar organisation in the world and its revelations did much, by convincing the Americans of German intrigues in U.S.A., to pave the way for the United States' entry into the war.

'I cannot at the moment think of any man who has done more useful service in this war than you, and I salute you,' was the tribute which Colonel Edward House, President Wilson's envoy, paid to Admiral Hall.

The loss of the *Hampshire* resulted in belated improvements in security when planning the future movements of Very Important Personages in wartime. A blunder of similar magnitude was never repeated; in World War II the Prime Minister and other war leaders made far more dangerous journeys and undertook equally important missions without misadventure.

Many aspects of the death of Lord Kitchener remain a mystery and they are unlikely to be cleared up unless all relevant documents are made public. It is remarkable that far greater secrecy is still preserved on matters appertaining to World War I than World War II. Not only are many official papers and documents of the first war still on the secret list, but an equally large number of private papers of statesmen of the period are 'closed' to the researcher. The Balfour Papers in the British Museum are a typical example, and Balfour, it will be noted, was First Lord of the Admiralty at the time of the *Hampshire* disaster.

Indications are that many of these documents will not be available for inspection for many years to come. By then it may not be possible to assess their usefulness because many contemporary figures will have passed away. So this book may still not be the final assessment of a strange story.

BIBLIOGRAPHY

ARTHUR, Sir George: *Life of Lord Kitchener*, 1920.

BALLARD, Colin R.: *Kitchener*.

HODGES, Arthur: *Lord Kitchener*, 1936.

HAUSHOFER, Karl: *Kitchener*, 1934.

GERMAINS, Victor W.: *The Truth About Kitchener*, 1925.

WATTEVILLE, Dr. Herman G.: *Lord Kitchener*, 1939.

EVERWIEN, M.: *Ein Feldmarschall fährt in den Tod.*, 1938.

BLEY, W.: *Die Weltkriegsspionage*, 1931.

CARL, Ernst: *One Against England*, 1934.

MARQUARDT, E.: *Kitchener*, 1948.

ADMIRALTY WHITE PAPER Cmd. 2710. (Concerning the loss of H.M.S. *Hampshire*), 1926.

ALA MANA: *The Message: Lord Kitchener Lives*, 1922.

WOOD, Clement: *The Man Who Killed Kitchener*, 1932.

COURTNEY, Charles: *Unlocking Adventure*, 1951.

PHILLIPS, William C.: *The Loss of H.M.S. Hampshire*, 1930.

JELLICOE OF SCAPA, Admiral Viscount: *The Grand Fleet: 1914–16*, 1919.

PARLIAMENTARY PAPER Cmd. 1068 (Battle of Jutland), Appendix III, 1920.

DER KRIEG ZUR SEE: Nordsee, Band V (The German Official History of World War I at sea).

MCADIE, A. G.: *War Weather Vignettes*.

CHURCHILL, Winston S.: *World Crisis*.

JONES, Dr. Thomas: *Lloyd George*.

BURBIDGE, W. F.: *Wizard of Wales*.

GEORGE, David Lloyd: *War Memoirs*.

THOMSON, Malcolm: *David Lloyd George*.

GARDINER, A. G.: *Prophets, Priests & Kings*.

YOUNG, Filson: *With the Battle Cruisers*.

THOMSON, Sir Basil: *Queer People*.

HALDANE OF CLOAN, Viscount: *Richard Burdon Haldane: An Autobiography*.

MILLIS, Walter: *Road to War*.

ASQUITH, Margot: *Autobiography*.

SPENDER, J. A. and ASQUITH, Cyril: *The Life of Lord Oxford & Asquith*.

OXFORD AND ASQUITH, the Earl of: *Memories & Reflections*.

ROBERTSON, Field Marshal Sir William: *From Private to Field Marshal*.

JAMES, Admiral Sir William: *The Eyes of the Navy*, 1955.

Also consulted: The Correspondence of Dr. Walter Page, U.S. Ambassador to the United Kingdom in World War I; German Naval documents of World War I; Hansard and the following newspapers and periodicals: *The Times, Daily Telegraph, Daily Express, Daily Mail, Sunday Express, Sunday Referee, Sunday Chronicle, Daily Sketch, Daily Dispatch, Manchester Guardian, La Lumière, Temps, London Gazette, Neuste Nachrichten, New York Times, The Globe, Berliner Illustrierte Zeitung, Morning Post, Evening Standard, Stavangeren, Belfast News, Volkischer Beobachter*.

INDEX

A

Abwehr, 118, 186, 209, 213

Abwehr II, 212, 213

Admiralty White Paper, Cmd 2710, 29, 55, 59, 61, 62, 63, 67, 68, 72, 74, 86, 87, 88, 90, 139, 140, 141, 152, 153, 155, 164, 165, 191, 192, 202, 203, 204, 205, 207

Aitken, Max (Lord Beaverbrook), 79

Alexander, Rev. P. G., 48

Alouette, 13

Amberger, Korvetten-Kapitan Gustav, 156, 157, 159

Angus, Joe, 41, 42, 43, 54, 56, 59

Arthur, Sir George, 10, 11, 79, 87, 89, 90, 95, 97, 122, 128, 191, 193

Asquith, H. H., 80, 83, 84, 94, 95, 96, 103, 119, 120, 122, 123

Asquith, Miss Elizabeth, 84

Asquith, Mrs., 83, 84, 119

Audacious, H.M.S., 161

B

Balfour (Lord), A. J., 96

Balfour Papers, 217

Barthe, Monsieur, 187

Beatty, Admiral Sir David, 215

Beitzen, Ober-Leutnant Kurt, 147, 150, 152, 154, 156, 157, 183

Bellairs, Commander, 123

Bennet, Warrant Mechanician W. M., 66, 70

Blake, H.M.S., 76

Bley, W., 166, 167, 174, 206

Boissier, Lt., R.M.A., 62, 73

Borkowski, Capt., 165, 166

Bowman, Able Seaman J. R., 64, 66, 70

Bridgeman, W. C., 89, 125, 126, 128, 129, 130, 201

Brock, Vice-Admiral Sir F. E., 45, 54, 58

Brooke, Lt.-Col., R.M.A., 61

Broome Hall, 110, 114

Broome, Viscount, 203

Brown, Driver D. C., 11

Buerdsell, Able Seaman H. Ll., 70

Burbidge, W. F., 95

Burnden, Alfred, 9, 10, 11

C

Cambodia, 54, 55, 59

Cameronia, 85

Carl, Ernst (see Gelrichsheimer), 171–7, 198, 211, 212

Carson, Sir Edward, 81, 103

Casement, Sir Roger, 105, 112, 176, 194

Cashman, Leading Seaman W., 70

Chattopadhya, 113

Churchill, Winston (Sir), 80, 92, 93

City of Selby, 59

Comité des Forges, 186

Comloquoy, Miss Jessie, 54

Cooper, Sir Richard, 123, 124, 126, 127, 140, 175

Courtney, Charles, 178–90

Cox, E. F., 189

Creedy, Sir Henry, 11, 35

Curzon of Kedleston, Marquess, 101

D

D'Albuquerque, Monsieur, 188, 190

Dalziel, Sir Henry (see also Dalziel, Lord), 123, 141, 198

Dalziel, Lord, 116

Dartmouth, H.M.S., 18

Davenport, Guilles, 185

Davies, Skipper, 73

S

Sabiston, Mr. John, 75
Sabiston, Mrs., 64, 65, 74
Savill, Capt. Herbert J., 19, 20, 21, 24, 25, 26, 31, 32, 33, 35, 40, 41, 202, 208, 209
Savinkov, Monsieur, 91, 92
Scherp, Korvetten-Kapitan, 157
Schmidt, Dr. Paul, 168
Scrymgeour, Mr., 128, 129
Simonovitch, Aron, 99, 100
Simpson, Able Seaman R., 64, 70
Sims, Stoker F. L., 70
Sinclair, Mr. J. G., 57, 58, 61
Soudan, H.M.S., 20, 72
Star of Dundee, 125
Stein, Johann George, 181
Stewart, Lieut.-Cdr. F. G., 48
St. Magnus, 137
Stoermer, Otto, 118, 159, 186, 187, 209, 210, 211, 212
Surguy-Shields, Henry, 11
Swaffer, Hannen, 78, 85
Sweeney, Petty Officer S. E., 27, 66, 70, 75, 199, 208

T

Tarpin, René, 161
Tasker, Major R. I., 129, 130, 191, 192
Tennant, H. J., 103
Tennyson, 169, 170
Thomas, Albert, 186, 187
Thomas, Lowell, 117
Thomson, Mr. Malcolm, 95, 121
Thomson, Sir Basil, 103, 106, 113, 116
Thomson, G. L., 56, 57, 58, 60

U

Unity, H.M.S., 23, 24, 25, 26, 58, 59

V

Vance, Detective-Inspector, 192–204, 207, 214
Victor, H.M.S., 23, 24, 25, 26, 58, 70
Von Glasenapp, Korvetten-Kapitan, 157, 159
Von Scheer, Admiral, 149, 153, 215

W

Walker, Capt. D. M., R.N., 54, 55, 57, 58
Waterhouse, Capt., 125
Watt, Mrs., 67
Weiss, Dr. Erwin, 119, 168, 209
Weissfelt, Max, 182, 183
Wesson, Petty Officer W., 23, 27, 28, 30, 32, 36, 37, 38, 49, 50, 51, 59, 66, 69, 70
Wetzell, General, 16, 98
Williams, Wythe, 116, 117
Wilhelm, Kaiser, 83
Wilson, Field Marshal Sir Henry, 101
Wilson, President Woodrow, 96
Wood, Clement, 169

Y

Young, Filson, 161

Z

Zaharoff, Sir Basil, 178, 181, 184, 185, 186, 187, 188, 190
Zaza, 59
Zippser, Harold, 184